*CITI*works

and

The 5% Solution Strategy

An economic plan to use
the 'Black Dollar' and black businesses
to revitalize American cities

By Joseph R. Hudson

To those who made this book possible, thank you

This book is the result of life lessons I have learned from the many people I have met in fulfilling civic responsibilities in the black community at the local, state and federal level, from those with whom I have worked and from those who have coached me in business. To each of you, please accept a heart-felt thank you for the various ways in which you have influenced my thinking. Some of you have touched my life in very special ways.

First to God, from whom all blessing flow, praise your Holy name! Next is my dear friend, coach, mentor, and confidant, William Charles Jameson, former Executive Director of the Interracial Council for Business Opportunity in Washington, D.C. Among the many others who have helped me reach the conclusions you will read in the following pages are: My former boss, William Schaffer, and colleagues at American Security and Trust Company in Washington, D.C. who took a chance on employing their first black male employee as a teller; Malcolm Corrin, President of the Interracial Council for Business Opportunity (ICBO) in New York City; Charles Kelley, Hugh Dash, Pat Ouisley and Sharon Fleming Owens at ICBO Atlanta; James "Butch" Beverly, ICBO New Orleans (recently deceased); the Board of Directors of the Interracial Council for Business Opportunity of Atlanta; the Honorable Winfred Dukes, Charles Johnson and Lonnie Saboor of the Georgia Summit of African American Business Organizations (GSAABO); Gail Reeves, Sharon Hill, and the family of the Georgia Minority Supplier Development Council; Harriet Michel, Steve Sims, and the entire staff of the office of the National Minority Supplier Development Council in New York City; Nathaniel R. Goldston, Chairman of Gourmet Services in Atlanta; Al Anderson of Anderson Communications in Atlanta; civil rights hero Rev. Joseph E. Lowery; former Atlanta Mayors Maynard Holbrook Jackson (deceased), Andy Young, Shirley Franklin, and Bill Campbell; the educational staff at the Minority Business Development Education School Amos Tuck School at Dartmouth College; Franklin O'Neal and Leona Barr Davenport of the Atlanta Business League; and the Rev. Byron Thomas and Rev. Fredrick Gray of Central United Methodist Church in Atlanta. Friends and personal debaters, Mack Wilbourn, Brenda Branch, Norman Holmes, Marian Stallworth, Sam Young, Yvonne Garret, Ralph Wright, Paula Valentine, Phil Johnson and Richard Finley; business associates, Henry Whitlow, B. Kirk Patterson, Edwin Bethea, Wendell Love, and the hundreds of clients who utilize our services at the Hudson Strategic Group; and early mentors Ted Hagans and Berkley Burrell at the National Business League in Washington, D.C.

Most of all I want to thank the most indescribably supportive and patient woman I know, Marsha Sampson Johnson, for her love and encouragement through the years as I researched and wrote this book. I also owe a special thanks to my wonderful family, starting with my Mother, Mattie Rose Hudson, my Father, Dewitt Hudson, my brothers and sister, and "the village" that raised me in Aliquippa, Pennsylvania. Finally, through the thoughts expressed in this book, I hope I am passing on to my hero, my son, Gregory, and his family, and my daughter, Sabrina, the realization that the sum of their experiences will only become recognized and have lasting value when they apply them to the public good.

Special acknowledgement

Thomas A. Oder of Worldwide Editing contributed writing and editing services for this book.

Worldwide Editing is an Atlanta company that specializes in providing writing, editing, and related services such as media relations to a diverse group of academics, entrepreneurs, and multinationals in the Americas, Europe, and Asia. Mr. Oder, created Worldwide Editing after retiring from Atlanta-based Cox Newspapers in 2008.

Contents

Section one

Why I wrote this book

"We've got to help ourselves – the cavalry ain't coming."
Joseph Hudson

Chapter one: There's a gold mine in the ghetto   Page 10
"The future is already here, it is just not evenly distributed."
William Gibson

American cities have been in decline for 30 years. Nowhere is that decline more obvious than in the inner city, which tends to be poor, black and "the ghetto" to some. City revitalization plans often call for these communities to be torn down. This book takes the opposite view. I believe there is a gold mine of black spending power in the inner city. I wrote this book as an economic plan, not a social plan, to show how black businesses can mine that gold. The premise of this plan, called *CITI*works and The 5% Solution Strategy, is that black businesses can lead a revival of the inner city that will re-vitalize the entire city and that this can happen all across America.

Section two

How the black community got to where it is today

"Difficulty is not an obstacle, it is merely an attribute."
Wal Sakaluk

Chapter one: A historical perspective   Page 15
"You never take a fence down till you know why it was built."
Anonymous

After the Civil War, the freed slaves migrated to the North and Midwest where they formed cities within cities. During what would become a prolonged struggle for equality, these enclaves became bastions of an embattled people. Even so, they were thriving, vibrant places. A hundred years later, the Civil Rights movement of the 1960s opened doors that allowed black businesses and black people to move to the suburbs. This migration led to several unintended consequences of integration. One was that the economic structure that had knitted the inner city together disappeared. Another was that the black community became a market instead of a place. As a result of these demographic shifts, the historic identity of the inner city vanished. The black community has struggled to regain its economic vitality and identity ever since.

Chapter two: The inner-city black community   Page 20
"It takes a village to raise a child."
African proverb

For 400 years, a variety of laws denied blacks economic power. Even though those laws have been repealed, blacks are still struggling for economic equality. Today, a disproportionate number of black-owned vs. white-owned businesses and a smorgasbord of entitlement programs have left blacks as de facto properties of the state rather than large landowners. Until now, no agreed-upon economic strategy has been offered to show how blacks can shake off these modern-day shackles. *CITI*works and The 5% Solution Strategy offer a plan to bring back the vitality of the black inner city – without the segregation.

Chapter three: The black business landscape   Page 26
"You can't tear down the master's house using the master's tools."
Anonymous

*CITI*works and The 5% Solution Strategy seek to change the language and results about corporate and government contracts with black business. The talk until now has been about social consciousness. This book changes the language to economics and how investing in the black community can lead to jobs, wealth creation, and civic and educational improvements.

Chapter four: The black experience has created a unique black market. Page 31
*"Success is not the result of spontaneous combustion.
You must set yourself on fire."*
Fred Shero

Black people have had a unique cultural and civic experience in America. Their experience has created a black market that is unique to the black community. The secret to realizing the full potential of this market lies in five capabilities that are distinct to black life and culture. When these capabilities are developed into a *CITI*works plan and implemented through The 5% Solution Strategy, they have the ability to raise the profile of the black market and make it even more powerful than it already is.

Chapter five: America's taboo subject ... race. Page 37
"I have learned that success is to be measured not so much by the position that one has reached in life as by the obstacles overcome in trying to succeed.
Booker T. Washington

Any issue related to race causes many communities to struggle with complex emotions and historical baggage. *CITI*works and The 5% Solution Strategy say we must get past this and have an honest discussion about the most taboo topic in the country. And that doesn't mean being color blind.

Section three

A call to action! *CITI*works and the 5% Solution Strategy

"We cannot solve our problems with the same level of thinking that created them."
Albert Einstein

Chapter one: A black blueprint Page 42
"A good system shortens the road to the goal."
Orison Marden

Even against a backdrop of history and despair, assets are in place in the inner city to create vibrant economic activity that will turn over the 'black dollar' multiple times before that dollar exits the city. The "Black Blueprint" of *CITI*works and The 5% Solution Strategy harnesses black spending power by asking blacks to commit to spending an additional 5 percent year-over-year with black businesses and groups. This spending will stimulate and support black employment and the development of black communities in which these businesses are located. The blueprint to increase black business activity can be applied in any city and, as its guidelines are followed, will lead to a resurgence of not only the inner city but the city as a whole.

Chapter two: The return on the investment Page 50
"Why not go out on a limb? That's where the fruit is."
Will Rogers

*CITI*works and The 5% Solution Strategy are not built on emotion or conjecture. Rather, they are built with a business plan and pre-set goals so that stakeholders can use economic indicators to measure the return on their investment. The ROI in this model reallocates resources to create value for the entire city in the form of new businesses and jobs, philanthropy, black business growth, civic leadership, and a full gamut of infrastructure improvements.

Chapter three: *CITI*works is the inexhaustible engine   Page 55
"Write the vision and make it plain so that ALL who read can run with it."
Habakkuk 2:2

There is a saying that *"when the black community works, the entire city works."* *CITI*works makes both the black community *and* the entire city work because it recognizes that the assets to achieve the plan's goals are already in place in the form of black businesses and black purchasing power. As a business model, *CITI*works serves as a toolkit that leverages these assets through the 5 percent spending formula and turns them into long-term economic activities that produce new and continuing transactions with visible results.

Chapter four: The 5% Solution Strategy   Page 66
"You have to cut the garment to fit the cloth."
John Cox

While the premise of The 5% Solution Strategy calls on blacks to spend an additional 5 percent year-over-year with black businesses, *CITI*works is not a cookie-cutter approach to revitalizing inner-city communities. The *CITI*works model and 5 percent strategy were developed with the awareness that every inner-city is different, that the black leadership in each city knows what their needs and values are, and therefore they should be the ones to apply the model so that it best benefits their community. In recognizing that each inner city is different, The 5% Solution Strategy emphasizes that this uniqueness is a community's competitive advantage over other communities and offers ideas for the black community to capitalize on this advantage in measurable ways.

Chapter five: Call to Action! Implementing the CITIworks plan and 5% Solution Strategy   Page 78
"In any moment of decision, the best thing you can do is the right thing, the next best thing is the wrong thing, and the worst thing you can do is nothing."
Anonymous

*CITI*works and The 5% Solution Strategy can be put into action through a seven-step implementation process. This chapter explains that process in detail. One of the most important of these steps is to create a campaign to educate everyone in the black community that *CITI*works is an economic plan, not a social plan, and that it does not involve entitlements. With this understanding, the leadership team is ready to articulate the results that the plan will produce and how those results will revitalize not only the inner-city community but the entire city, which is the ultimate goal of *CITI*works.

Section four

What others are saying   Page 86

"At the end of the day, what is good for black communities and all communities of color, strengthens the American economy and allows the United States to remain globally competitive."
Daryl Williams – Kauffman Foundation

Experts in racial relations put the plight and potential of the black community and black spending power into perspective.

Section five

Statistical Data   Page 89

"You can't lead the Calvary if you think you look funny on a horse"."
Anonymous

Census and academic research data show in hard numbers the impact that *CITI*works and The 5% Solution Strategy can have in revitalizing America's cities.

Economic empowerment

Is it threatening? Views have changed.

In 1969, George Meany, then president of the AFL-CIO, said this:

"At its worst, 'black capitalism' is a dangerous, divisive delusion – offered as a panacea by extremists, both black and white. Attempts to build economic enclaves with substantial federal tax subsidies within specific geographically limited ghetto areas is apartheid, anti-democratic nonsense.

Almost 30 years later, on May 25, 1998, this statement appeared in the Washington Post.

"Any group that does not have an economic structure is heading for trouble. The groups that hold the most control over their financial, human capital and markets will be the most competitive groups."

CITIworks utilizes the black business

as the inexhaustible economic engine of the inner city!

Chapter 1

There's a gold mine in the ghetto

"The future is already here, it's just not evenly distributed."
William Gibson

I have devoted my life's work to the economic development of the black business community. In 40-plus years as a business owner, as a leader on numerous boards and councils, as a member of civic groups that gathered in meeting rooms at neighborhood churches and business associations sponsored by the White House, as a foot soldier in the political arena, as a non-profit black business development executive, and as a researcher of black life in America, I have experienced the struggles of black-owned businesses on a professional and intensely personal level. These experiences have led me to a deeply held conviction that black-owned businesses can become the economic engines that drive the revival of inner-city black communities across America. The resurgence of the inner city is important to more than just these core municipal enclaves. Our cities have been in decline for 30 years. Black businesses, in my view, are the key to stopping that decline. I believe that reversing the trend and regenerating the business and cultural vibrancy of the inner city also will lead to a revival of the entire city. This, I am convinced, can happen all across America. I wrote this book to show how black businesses can lead this resurgence.

It is not of critical importance, in my view, whether the black business is located in the inner city or in the suburbs. Wherever they are located, black businesses have shown that by their nature they employ more black people than people of other races or ethnicities. As a result, black people have the ability to increase black-to-black spending in the black community. There is a proven premise for such a spending pattern: People have an affinity for people of the same heritage. Employment and spending choices happen for this very reason in the Hispanic, Indian, and Asian communities. This book shows how the black community can create not only jobs but wealth, philanthropy, entrepreneurs, and black civic leadership.

The thoughts expressed in this book are a compilation of the beliefs and views I have formed from the many speeches I have heard, the discussions I have had with numerous friends, and from what I have learned in leading and directing entrepreneurs of all ages, types, and business classifications. This book is intended to bring into context the story of a people, their struggle for respect, and the opportunity that is within their grasp to fulfill their potential by thinking of black businesses as an economic generator. While this book contains many well-founded generalizations, the conclusions reached in the book are supported with comments from subject matter experts who have far more knowledge about the economic development of the black business community than I do. Where appropriate, these conclusions are supported with statistics. However, the reader will not find the book filled with charts and graphs of data. When telling the story of a people, in this case the story of black business men and women and the black community in America, I believe the best way to tell that story is not with numbers from an accounting ledger but through the passion of words, thoughts and ideas that express achievable hopes and dreams.

The path that led to this book

I was educated at Howard University, Stanford University, the Wharton School of Business, the Darden School of Business Amos Tuck School, and the London School of Business. I have traveled a path that has led me from being a banker, to a black business developer, to a black business owner, to a corporate-minority organizational executive, to a non-profit board member and business/organizational/community consultant to where I am today – an advisor, coach, and business strategist. I have been an active community partner, chairing or serving on more than 30 non-profit boards of directors, including the Atlanta Downtown Development Authority, Fulton County (Georgia) Department of Family And Children's Services, and The Georgia Black United Fund. I have represented small business on the White House Conference on Small Business, The Region 4 U.S. Small Business Administration, and The State of Georgia Small Business Study Commission. I have served as president and CEO of The Interracial Council for Business Opportunity, co-founded and became president of the Georgia Minority Supplier Development Council, and have been a participant in Leadership Atlanta and the Regional Leadership Institute.

Other experiences have helped to broaden my perspective about the role black businesses can play in revitalizing America's cities. I have participated in the White House Program on Executive Exchange, where I served as a "Presidential Exchange Executive." I have testified before the U.S. Small Business Subcommittee of Congress and have been a small business newspaper columnist for three newspapers. I also have experienced the ups and downs of entrepreneurship by owning four businesses. Currently, I am the founder and Chairman of the Hudson Strategic Group, which provides strategic planning and organizational services to non-profits, private enterprises, governments, and community organizations. I was fortunate to acquire additional skills as a fellow in the International Business Fellow Program, as a participant in the Department of Defense "Joint Civilian Orientation Conference," and in business-related global travel. Visits to several African countries, Japan, South Korea, and England have helped to round out my knowledge about the black business community and economic development.

Most recently, I facilitated the development of local strategic plans in seven Georgia cities that addressed the topic of "blacks doing business with blacks." Fortunately, I have been able to extend my knowledge about black business through my membership in the Atlanta Business League, where I have served as Vice Chair of Public Policy. In that role, I led the "The Congress on the State of Black Businesses" for the past six years. The Congress has taken on the subject of creating a method to address the economic depravation of the black community through a turnover strategy for the "Black Dollar." The six Congresses have brought together more than 1,500 people, ranging from key government officials such as the mayor of Atlanta, prominent black business owners, top non-profit and church leaders, to everyday small business owners and consumers as well as nationally known speakers and economists.

A business plan, not a social plan

This book speaks to what I have learned through these wide-ranging experiences, which is that a black community, by strategically focusing on a commonly developed plan, can begin to reach its full potential through the simple investment of black people using their purchasing power to buy products and services from black businesses. The book also addresses how the turnover of the "Black Dollar" can stimulate a community development effort that can be nurtured and encouraged over time and bring identifiable results.

There is an old saying: "If you put a dollar in, you can expect to get a dollar out!" That is the premise of this book. If the black community can take advantage of its natural resources and direct those resources into the economic mainstream of the black community through black-owned businesses, then the community can expect to get returns commensurate to its investment. In today's world, those who have grown dependent on government largess are receiving less and less support. The message is clear. The government is no longer the savior. Therefore, it is incumbent on black communities to move from depending upon entitlement programs to creating a sustainable economic model that provides a return on investment (ROI) that will sustain the desired lifestyle of the community and its members.

How can the black community do that?

My business partner, Henry Whitlow, created a concept to achieve this goal. Together, we've taken this concept and enlarged it to include a strategic "Black Blueprint" that addresses community development and black business opportunity by empowering black businesses to become the inexhaustible engine of the inner city. We have named this "Black Blueprint" *CITI*works. *CITI*works enables the black community in cities across America through their own input to design a plan for how they want their community to be in the future. The *CITI*works concept allows and even encourages communities to utilize other programs and resources to drive their plan to achieve the community's desired outcome. The underlying principle of *CITI*works is an action plan called The 5% Solution Strategy. Simply put, this strategy is a long-term effort that calls on black people to re-invest in their community by spending an additional 5 percent year after year with black-owned businesses. In its essence, The 5% Solution Strategy leverages all of the assets of the black community – people, businesses, organizations, etc. – in a self-help type manner to achieve the goals of *CITI*works.

In Section III, Chapter 4, I list 10 reasons why *CITI*works and The 5% Solution Strategy can help revive not only black inner cities but cities as a whole. These reasons offer a guideline to reverse the long-held negative view of inner cities and to see them in a new light as goldmines of opportunity. *CITI*works and The 5% Solution Strategy offer a plan for black businesses to mine that gold!

I realize this is exactly the opposite perception of inner-city black communities. The answer to the problem of inner cities – the ghetto, to some – too often has been to tear them down in the name of gentrification and regionalization. As a result, black businesses have been forsaken in an unstated policy of "throw the baby out with the bath water." *CITI*works and The 5% Solution Strategy offer a plan to show how black business can re-create entire cities to everyone's mutual benefit by re-creating the value of the inner-city black community.

Will our theory work when put into practice in the "real world" of real cities and real people? Yes. How can we be so sure? Because the ideas on which *CITI*works are based have been successfully tested for a period of eight years in Atlanta and six other Georgia cities. The Atlanta Business League has embraced The 5% Solution Strategy and was already implementing it even as this book was being written.

Section two

How the black community got to where it is today

"Difficulty is not an obstacle, it is merely an attribute."
Wal Sakaluk

Chapter

1

A historical perspective

"You never take a fence down 'til you know why it was built."
Anonymous

In the years after the Civil War, the freed slaves migrated from the South to the North and Midwest where they formed cities within cities. These enclaves became communities that sociologists and urban planners would come to call the black inner city. Others, not so kindly, would call them "the ghetto." In city after city where black folks settled, even though these communities didn't have walls or defined borders they became safe havens for the enterprises and activities of a race of people who sought ways to take care of themselves and each other. Within these communities, black entrepreneurs began forming businesses and black people began creating new lives, getting by as well they could. Over time, these inner-city communities became bastions emblematic of the embattled minority who lived in them and who struggled to survive individually and collectively and to compete for a place in society. These times are frequently cited in historical literature as what capitalism was all about — the self-production of jobs, social structure, and enterprise.

In the years after the Civil Rights movement of the 1960s, black businesses began expanding to the suburbs and pursuing sales and providing services throughout their cities and regions. While integration began opening doors that had long been closed to blacks, it produced several unintended consequences. For one, the economic structures and tools that knitted the fabric of the inner city together disappeared. For another, the black community became a *market* of people, not a *place* where people lived. Before long, the historic identity of the black inner-city vanished. The black community, no longer at least partially confined by loose geographic boundaries nor defined by them, has struggled to regain its economic vitality and its identity ever since.

This brief historical overview is not meant to disregard any of the challenges presented by racism or the political conditions of the times. During the many decades of segregation, racial attitudes were so severe they not only limited opportunities for blacks but in fact denied them many of the rights to even exist. The point is that in spite of the denial of equal rights to black people, black communities in the century between the end of the Civil War and the Civil Rights movement were thriving, vibrant places despite the times and the conditions. In fact, especially given the circumstances during those 100 years, in some cities some black businesses became so successful that they created resentment among white business and civic leaders. This resentment led business and political leaders in the larger community to take many unfair, and ultimately unproductive, actions to dismantle black enclaves. They wanted these communities to go away! Black people obliged by trying to become fully integrated into the white society outside of their historical community.

Black businesses enter the economic mainstream

In the years after this sea change in the demographics of American cities, black businesses were neither recognized nor credited with the opportunities they had created. That, of course, didn't mean their successes had not happened. It meant that the successes became disguised. In a more important sense, black businesses and their achievements became invisible. The implication was that personal and business opportunities only existed in and according to the rules of the larger white community. In effect, the message to the black community was that it was devoid of economic activity, and the only way for black businesses to have success was for them to be like the businesses of the "white folks." The impact on the black community, to its great detriment, was for blacks to believe that black businesses did not exist as a means for success, recognition or importance.

As time passed, the federal government realized that it was politically important for black businesses to become an integral part of the mainstream economic vitality of the United States. As a result, assistance programs were created to help blacks and other minorities gain a foothold in the business system. These efforts, while designed to stimulate minority involvement in the commerce of the country, reassigned the leadership of the black community to primarily black businesses, civil rights leaders, and black ministers by default.

Because people of similar ethnic and racial backgrounds have an affinity to live, work and play in close proximity to each other, the black community has continued to exist, albeit not as an enclave within loosely defines boundaries in cities but as a community of people. During the early days of the Civil Rights movement, the white community, through local government and businesses, began providing support and undergirding the activities of the black community in general. This produced another unintended result of integration. The black community became dependent upon the economic support of the majority white community through a smorgasbord of assistance programs known as "entitlements."

Since the mid-1990s, support provided by these programs has been declining. Black businesses are now being required to step up and recreate the type of economic communities and models for the development of the black community that are, in effect, shadow models of the ones from segregation days.

The modern black business community

Where does this leave the black community today, a little more than a decade into the 21st century? Black communities have, in fact, been recreated, but not as the solitary island communities that once existed in the larger white communities. They have been recreated as a market. In this case, though, the market is not a place. It is a people! The market exists because black people through their culture and values have utilized non-traditional methods to achieve economic success. Additionally, because blacks have created a market, they are the ones who hold the keys to tap into that market. The lesson for everyone of all ethnicities and races is that the affinity of a people for each other and their desire to explore and exploit opportunities inherent to them as equal members of the human family cannot be denied.

Affinity groups are nothing new. They have existed in cities across America since Irish, German, Polish or other nationalities left Europe, Asia or other nations or regions to escape a variety of crises and build new lives in the New World. We mostly know these separate ethnic areas of American cities as German Towns, China Towns or Korea Towns or "towns" where the majority of the residents are of Indian, Russian or Eastern European origin. These "towns" within towns, or cities within cities, are known for their distinctive food, for the appeal of their native cultures and for attracting tourists. But nowhere in America, according to Dr. Claud Anderson, president of The Harvest Institute, a non-profit, tax-exempt nationally recognized black think tank that works to help Black America become a self-sufficient and competitive group of people, do you find a "Black Town." There are, however, black communities that exist for the same affinity reasons that have created ethnic "towns."

These black communities were formed as a direct result of the marches for Civil Rights, passage of Civil Rights laws, opening of schoolhouse doors to public education for blacks that was equal to the education available to whites, and the realization of economic possibilities for black citizens through access to the same job opportunities as whites. Then in the late 1970s and '80s, federal, city, and state governments passed legislation that gave black businesses new opportunities to grow and to prosper. The changes in federal laws spurred other initiatives, such as Disparity Studies, that were created to lend credence to efforts to assist black business development. Corporations took notice of these programs and joined the effort to support black business development through what is now known as Supplier Diversity programs. The banking community became even more responsive to needs of the black community when Congress passed the Community Reinvestment Act (CRA) of 1977. This act reduced redlining, a discriminatory credit practice that targeted moderate and low-income neighborhoods.

While funding has been, and seemingly always will be, a problem for small black businesses, new sources of funding began to appear through the U.S. Small Business Administration and other sources. Today, for example, black businesses are able to take advantage of the "idle money" of angel investors and others. These funds are not universally available to every black business, but they are available and have opened doors to black entrepreneurs that include franchise models, joint ventures, and alliances with larger businesses. Finally, there are programs that were created to increase minority and small business participation in international commerce. Black-owned businesses are not participating in these programs at the same ratio as white-owned businesses, but there are black businesses that do take advantage of this growth opportunity. All of these changes in laws, culture, racial attitudes, government programs, and funding have begun to produce the modern-day black business employer. As a result, the black business community is growing and producing jobs at a record-breaking pace.

Ultimately, these changes, coupled with open housing, labor improvements and other societal changes, have led me to the view of the black community that I hold today. That view is that black businesses are no longer restricted to certain enclaves within cities. The 21st century black business in America is located almost anywhere the black entrepreneur determines he or she wants it to be. And, even though black communities still exist as clusters and, in my opinion, probably will always exist as an affinity group, the individual black business is no longer confined to "the ghetto." In fact, in this changing business and social environment, many black businesses are now starting out "at scale" to their market while others are growing to scale as their market dictates. Plus, the new back entrepreneur has a mindset that enables him or her to "to deal" with the market place in which they are offering their product or service.

My view also is that while there may no longer be a specific black community confined to well-known boundaries within cities, black businesses create the same economic benefit for blacks, particularly through job creation, wherever they are located. Black businesses regardless of their location, for example, will still be composed of an employee base that is two-thirds black, according to Danny Boston, a professor of economics in the School of Economics at

Georgia Tech and CEO of EuQuant, an economic research company that specializes in business analytics and urban planning.

The customer base may change because black businesses may be located in white communities, but it does not dissolve the requirements for black business owners to provide personal services or engage in relationships which may only exist for the most part within the inner city and the historically traditional black community. Additionally, black business owners still will continue to look to other black business owners for support and will continue to contribute to black-related causes.

Blacks now hold the keys to their future

Black communities must also recognize that blacks now hold the key prerequisites for success, not only for black businesses but for the black community as a whole. Blacks, for example, hold the vast majority of seats in city and local governments. Their dominance in elected leadership roles through the balkanization of America's core urban communities has given blacks control of many municipal infrastructures. Additionally, the level of education and pools of other resources, including money, while not yet comparable to the levels in white communities but available as a seed resource, are at historic high levels in black communities.

The challenge for blacks is to recognize that they hold these keys to the economic engines of urban communities and that they can turn these engines on by re-investing in black communities through the turnover of the "Black Dollar." If the black community will recognize and embrace this theory, then black businesses will become the economic generator they always sought to be rather than recipients of entitlements. When this happens, black business men and women will shatter the philosophical and institutional myth that black businesses are dependent on support from the larger community to survive and new doors will open to them to become community development leaders in a nationwide movement that will revive America's cities.

Chapter 2

The inner-city black community

"It takes a village to raise a child."
African proverb

The system we call capitalism has become twisted into a tool that supports and maintains the status quo. The idea that everyone – even the best and brightest black teenagers – should go to college so they can get a job has been firmly planted in the black community. On the surface, this message has merits. What's not been said, though, is just as important as what has been said. That is, black teens are not being encouraged to become entrepreneurs. By being programmed to seek jobs, they are not being encouraged to form businesses that would create wealth. Without wealth, a community and its people cannot attain their fair share of a nation's economic benefits.

During the past 400 years, state and local governments passed laws that denied blacks economic empowerment. Even though those laws have been repealed, their residual effect has had a lasting impact on the black community. That impact can be seen in a disproportionately low number of black-owned businesses compared to white-owned businesses. This has harmed the black community in two important ways. One, it has caused blacks to lack economic power. Two, it has caused black communities to become dependent on outside assistance for their well being. The result, even though blacks have been unshackled from the chains of slavery for 150 years, is that black people have in a sense become de facto "properties of the state" rather than the legal property of large landowners!

For black people to free themselves from this form of indentured servitude and for the black community to thrive, there is an urgent need for a new day in Black America. My quest to open the door of opportunity to that new day is where I discovered a fresh approach to community development. That approach is based on creating local strategies to encourage black people to do more business – spend more money! – with black businesses. Research, it should be pointed out, shows that only 2 percent of the black population works for black businesses, and that other minorities are now displacing blacks on the hierarchy of economic success.

Economists and Chambers of Commerce frequently promote small business as the backbone of the job-creation economy. Yet, efforts to create jobs are mostly directed at large companies. The thinking is that it is the big companies that have the capability to produce a large number of jobs at one time. Small businesses, on the other hand, may create only one or two jobs at a time, but they continually create them. There is another job-related benefit of small businesses. They don't downsize staff to improve profit margins or make investments work for their shareholders. Small businesses make investments in their services and products that work for the community in which they reside!

Black business owners have to deal not only with government lip service to small businesses, they also are saddled with negative racial perceptions in which they are viewed as inadequate. Even when they experience success, black entrepreneurs are made to seem invisible or are devalued in comparison to the higher profile of those who have a corporate position or, sometimes, even a blue collar job. Because schools as providers of education have a long-standing relationship with major job providers, they are reluctant to put anything in their curriculum that does not emphasize studying hard so that you can get a job when you graduate.

The current status is what it is. We can only change that status by recognizing this truism and by dealing with it on that basis. *CITI*works and The 5% Solution Strategy accept this distinction and say don't deny it. But at the same time, the goal is to change the paradigm and bring attention to the outcomes.

The goal is wealth as well as jobs

Research shows that minority-owned businesses have a tendency to hire more minority employees than non-minority owned firms. The U.S. Small Business Administration (SBA) agrees! It has taken the position that a minority hiring requirement would pose a burden for some companies because it would conflict with the agency's long-standing goal of creating entrepreneur opportunities. The SBA's position is that there is a need for a separate program that focuses specifically and directly on creating jobs and economic development in economically distressed communities. I have a name for that program. It's called *CITI*works and The 5% Solution Strategy!

Most inner-city residents have a theory about programs that result in businesses – black or white-owned – that get contracts in a city. They see these businesses as takers rather than givers. They believe that these businesses take resources from the city rather than put resources into it that will help the people who live there prosper. Residents see these businesses as faceless entities that play political games with city leaders because their chief concern is to create wealth for themselves rather than to produce wealth and lifestyle benefits for the community.

While these large companies do create jobs, the income from those jobs does not produce wealth except, possibly, for the lucky few who climb the corporate ladder into top leadership positions. The rank and file workers do not become wealthy. Thus, residents of inner-city communities don't accrue wealth from the presence of big businesses that locate in cities. In fact, over time, these communities actually regress.

History has shown that the black consumer and black businesses can be a self-sustaining market. It is a simple principle. The turnover of the "Black Dollar" creates additional opportunity for additional players. That's what happened in the days of segregation, and it can happen again.

Businesses located within a respective community, especially black businesses, provide an old-fashion way to address the needs of community. The recycling of the dollar creates a self-developed market. The idea is to permit a local inner-city community to take advantage of the turnover of the dollar within it before the dollar exits the community. All of the businesses within the community can support this principle including, with proper consideration, even corporations. It's just a "common sense" approach!

Absolutes, truths and myths

The approach I take throughout this book is that there are few absolutes about inner-city black communities and black businesses but there is a lot of truth. Facts are few because information about inner-city enclaves and black businesses most often are gathered through Census data. Therefore, there is a lag between when data is collected and when conclusions are reached. In that lag time, conditions change. What I am trying to do with *CITI*works and The 5% Solution Strategy is to create a model in which truths can be presented in real time so that conclusions previously reached can become the start of a new thought process, not the summary of thought.

This book addresses several myths. Among those are the many generalizations that have been reached about black and inner city businesses. Even the limited data that has been collected points to a different reality than exists in common perceptions. Also, this book offers a new perspective about valuing black businesses for the potential they have to regenerate America's cities by improving the conditions in inner-city black communities.

Thirty years of economic restructuring within American cities have had a marked effect on the black business market. Initially, the black community was weakened because it was left dependent on traditional government sectors and was slow to respond to new opportunities. It had become an economy dependent on large enterprises often employing many people. But these companies in many cases have relocated from the cities to the suburbs.

Inner cities also suffered because public money failed the black business community in two ways. First, it failed to foster and support entrepreneurial activity. Most programs that have been created to support black business activity have been in the form of benefits, regeneration (without strategy) and public services, a large part of which immediately leaks out of the local economy rather than supporting it. Second, public money has failed to create the right incentives to help generate the most powerful opportunities black business could have: Self-help and mutual aid. Sadly, other initiatives soon became fodder for those who considered these efforts entitlements and who attempted to discourage them at every turn.

It is perplexing that while black-owned and small businesses are credited with job growth and development, they are not actively included in the important things that a region must get right if it is to succeed over time. This sector has been ridiculed and assailed, as have other "minority" businesses, as a social parasite that does not contribute anything to a city but takes away from its value and appeal. Numbers tell a different story. An economic impact study conducted for the Atlanta Business League, for example, showed that black businesses in the Atlanta metropolitan area employ more than 56,000 people, cause the employment of an additional 126,000 people and have an overall economic impact of $24 billion.

Answering the *"what if"* question

It is time to increase the support for this sector through individual purchases, contracts, and financial support to enable the economic engine of the black business community to pull its own weight and lead the growth of America's inner cities. Black business leaders should also be included in economic leadership decisions by having a place at the table of civic decision-making. Their seat at this table should be one in which they represent the black business sector as a full partner rather than simply being offered a seat on the Board of Directors of a corporation just to add diversity to that Board. When black business leaders have a voice in decisions that impact the community, it makes it clear to all of the stakeholders that black businesses are important to the overall health and welfare of a metropolitan region rather than being a symbolic member of a Board.

Now is the time to sharpen black business strategy, help existing black-owned companies grow, adopt progressive legislative policies and collaborate across the region and state to set and achieve specific goals. The legal arm twisting that thwarts black business growth and development needs to stop. What's needed is the *CITI*works investment approach of blacks doing more business with black businesses to enable black businesses to accelerate their contributions to local and national economic growth.

What has been missing is a plan and an implementation strategy to bring this concept into reality. Until now, no one has offered a picture and a strategy that asks *"what if"* for the black community. *CITI*works and The 5% Solution Strategy change the paradigm because they ask:

- *What if* black businesses were used as an economic engine for development?
- *What if* black communities developed a basic strategic plan to address their situation?
- *What if* black communities then developed implementation strategies to bring the plan into fruition?
- *What if* the game was changed from social and civil rights outcomes (full integration into white markets) to economic outcomes?
- *What if* we went from discussions about causing transactions to happen to discussions about the result of transactions?
- *What if* you could see the economic result of all of these different efforts to grow and support black businesses?

This is what *CITI*works and The 5% Solution Strategy are about. They answer the *"what if"* questions with *"what can be"* answers. *CITI*works and The 5% Solution Strategy provide a guideline for showing how the black business community can lead our country down a path of economic stability by more effectively utilizing black economic resources.

Bring back the old days – without segregation

Until now, we have always seemed to speak about transactions by contractors, entrepreneurs, or institutions. Going forward, *CITI*works and The 5% Solution Strategy propose that we speak about the results of transactions and their undeniable economic benefits. If we can see and show the return on the transaction, such as job creation, as being beneficial to the whole community, and especially to the inner city communities in which these business reside, black business owners and the black community can begin to gain broader support.

But first black business owners will have to overcome long-standing prejudices against black businesses having even the potential to establish economic value and a reluctance at the federal level to develop overall strategic plans that acknowledge black businesses in a significant way. Second, our cities must develop and embrace long-range strategies that support the vision of *CITI*works and The 5% Solution Strategy to bring back the "old days" when black businesses were the backbone of the black community but without the segregation that came with those days! That leadership is largely missing from inner-city communities, and what is there is disrespected or under utilized.

*CITI*works and The 5% Solution Strategy offer a planning process that says black people have economic values and that black communities, while often poor, offer great potential. Finally, *CITI*works and The 5% Solution Strategy offer a way to discuss the economic value of the "Black Dollar" as a vehicle to create a new type of Return on Investment for America's cities by keeping "Black Dollars" in black hands as long as possible in order to create black wealth.

*CITI*works and The 5% Solution Strategy remove the negative stigma of the black business and the black community. Together, they offer a self-help approach to business and community development. By utilizing black business and the economic activities they can generate, these businesses can begin turning over "Black Dollars" that will grow not only businesses but communities as well.

So, The REAL QUESTION is: What can the black business and the black community PRODUCE that is of value? The answer: JOBS and economic vitality!

Chapter 3

The black business landscape

"You can't tear down the master's house using the master's tools."
Anonymous

The various programs that support black businesses, regardless of what some people might think about them, have led to a marked change in the black business community that has given black business owners the ability to help drive economic recovery.

What hasn't happened during these years of historical progress is for these businesses, their owners, or the support programs to receive any recognition of the overall benefit these programs have produced. For example, most of the support efforts are considered and spoken of independently. We talk of loans or contracts, but not of loans *and* contracts. We talk about banks being required to lend, governments being required to contract, and about the recognition of market objective pass-throughs, but we don't talk about these things *and* their positive economic impact. We talk about blacks benefitting from working in corporate and government environments, but we don't talk about these opportunities *and* how they can lead to increased education, skills enhancement, or the possibility of acquiring potential startup funds to launch new businesses. All of these things, and more, have created changes that have improved the lives of black people. Maybe these changes are not to everyone's liking. But, the changes have taken place *and* they have produced positive results!

The education and experience of black business owners have grown by leaps and bounds since the era of Civil Rights protests. Consider this: A recent study revealed that more than 60 percent of black business owners who do business with major corporations have at least one college degree and more than 15 percent have two degrees. These business owners also have more than eight years of experience in their chosen field, according to the study. Now consider how different these numbers are from statistics about black business owners of the 1950s and '60s.

Educational opportunities that have become available to blacks since the days of segregation have led to other changes in the demographics of black business owners and the black work force. Whereas black business models in the '50s, '60s and earlier were built around the owner's unique ability to work with his or her hands, blacks today are building business around the ability to work with their minds. And, finally, the black workforce is better educated than in past decades. As such, it is better positioned to assist both the sophisticated and unsophisticated black business owner. In some sectors, black businesses are still clearly better positioned to employ people considered unemployable or less-employable because the business may need less sophisticated employees than companies requiring high education levels or a record of previous employment.

Let's expand on the landscape for black businesses by looking at supplier diversity opportunities in corporate and supply chains.

Corporate and government supply chain programs

Supplier diversity is a business process in which governments and corporations actively source products and services from suppliers who previously have been under-used. Supplier diversity is considered a progressive process because it mirrors the demographics of the community in which the corporation operates by proactively seeking to do business with diverse suppliers. In time, a commitment to supplier diversity will transform a corporation's supply chain. In their current state, the various programs that have been created to implement and sustain supplier diversity are under constant attack. Top executives have targeted them for criticism because they see them as unnecessary and poorly managed affirmative action programs. According to this thinking, affirmative action is a helping-hand holdover from an era of segregation and discrimination that may no longer exists. It is true that in their infancy supplier diversity programs were dumping grounds. However, they have evolved into successful business management tools. In fact, supplier diversity programs may be the most obvious program to support *CITI*works through The 5% Solution Strategy and the easiest one to re-engineer into an effective tool to spur community economic development. To understand how that can happen, it's important to understand the history of supplier diversity.

During the late 1960s and '70s, blacks put political pressure on both federal and local governments to create programs designed primarily to grant blacks and other minorities equal access to purchasing opportunities. Since those early days of affirmative action, many groups have been added to the diversity mix. Women, veterans, disabled veterans, members of the LGBT community, historically under-utilized businesses and SBA-defined small business vendors are now eligible to seek government procurement opportunities through supplier diversity programs.

In those early years, the primary function of people and companies in the supplier diversity program was purchasing. The main goal was simply to buy products and services in an efficient manner that would keep organizations going – a task that was not thought of very highly. During the last 20 years, however, purchasing has gained respect. Purchasers have risen from a low rung on the corporate ladder to become an integral part of industry and government management teams. Purchasing as a business function has demonstrated its importance as supply chains have become increasingly complex and global and speed to market has become critical to business success. Purchasing managers are now responsible not only for global logistics as products and services move across borders and cultures but are also accountable as managers of outsourcing. At the same time when purchasing was being re-defined, Disadvantaged Business Programs (DBE) were being created and the role of suppliers was becoming more and more critical to the financial success of corporations and governments.

The problem today is that these programs too often are still stuck in the past. My company recently had the opportunity to evaluate how various levels of corporate executives viewed supplier diversity programs. What we found was not what corporations wanted to hear. Suppliers and the supplier coordinators generally thought the program was important, even if it accomplished only corporate introductions for the suppliers. Chief executives often had a different view. They tended to see supplier diversity as a complete "waste of time." In a few cases, sometimes along with the program coordinator, they held it in disdain – even though they might grudgingly admit it was an important accommodation to community relations. Why did they feel this way? The answer is simple. Money. Although purchasing departments and managers were "doing the right thing" and their efforts were socially responsible, purchasing as a business function did not generate revenue.

Finally, the tide appears to be turning. More and more corporate leaders are beginning to see the value of developing and using any supplier, including diversity suppliers. They want to show that they are sensitive to buyers and users of products. Perhaps even more importantly, minority suppliers are proving that they are as efficient, or even more efficient, than white suppliers. In that regard, corporations are beginning to reposition their supplier diversity programs. Most are even beginning to recognize that with a little effort and support they can develop minority suppliers into great suppliers. When this happens, company spokespersons invariably announce with great pride how much business – usually expressed in dollar amounts – they are doing with minorities.

Where does the community fit with supplier diversity?

Still, challenges remain. The effectiveness of supplier diversity programs have yet to reach their full potential. On one hand, in the effort to drive government contracts to minority businesses, the government too often merely verifies that the business is owned and operated by a minority without checking into how effectively the minority owner manages the business. On another, government programs have become political and are beginning to face the same realities with "ole black boy" suppliers as they did with "ole white boy" suppliers.

The most serious problem with these programs, however, goes much deeper than which black or minority business owners are awarded contracts. The real problem is that if any gain is derived from the contract, whether it's from a government or a corporation, that gain tends to go no further than the business or the business owner. The community, which is supposed to also be a beneficiary, does not see benefits from the contracts awarded under supplier diversity programs.

This is where The 5% Solution Strategy comes into play, especially the part that speaks to jobs and the results of transactions. Both corporations and governments have to move away from speaking about their efforts only in terms of contracting and procurement. In fact, I believe that form of identification brings about another unwanted result, which I call "personality contracting." This term refers to a business deal in which people suspect the business owner won the contract because he or she is a "favored child" rather than a capable supplier.

What's the issue?

The heart of the problem is language rather than function. Language is an issue for corporations and government because they continue to talk about supplier diversity in terms of social consciousness rather than financial opportunity and gain. The language they should be using is supplier *development*, not supplier diversity. The more effectively corporations and governments are able to identify and develop key suppliers the better they will find their chance of achieving their goals. In short, the conversation should be about ROI. Put another way, corporations and governments should ask themselves "how will choosing a particular supplier impact my bottom line?"

Currently, the language of procurement is expressed in the number of dollars procured from contracts. A better way to define return is in the number of jobs created. For one thing, this is something stakeholders and the public understand. For another, it expresses in business terms what the business is trying to accomplish.

The creation of jobs is especially important to the general population because the masses realize that this is a direct benefit to them. On another level, when procurement is expressed in economic terms, business people understand that certain economic instruments were used to achieve economic goals. In the case of *CITI*works and The 5% Solution Strategy, that instrument is black businesses.

Since black businesses tend to employ more blacks than non-blacks, are located near or within the black community and may not require people with high level skills, contracting with black businesses is – or, should be – a "no brainer," according to Boston. Even if the benefits are difficult to see and the results show up over time rather than immediately, Boston believes that with deliberate efforts the economic benefits will begin to emerge.

All this being said, the black community will support efforts that help it see positive benefits such as jobs, clean streets and better educational institutions. In addition, it makes it a great deal tougher to challenge DBE programs on their face if the outcomes expressed are economic and don't include the perception of entitlement.

Procurement to Build Capacity

Finally, as Boston says, "increasing the capacity and competitiveness of black-owned firms is the most important imperative for our community and country!"

Using contracting as a way to invest in black businesses helps the businesses build capacity and involves other key cultural and economic pillars of the black community such as financial institutions and community support. If used in this fashion, corporate and government contracts can be a major contributor to community development and the turnover of dollars, especially if viewed through the corrective lens of economic contributions rather than social responsibility and the right-thing-to-do mentality.

This new viewpoint also ties together the ability of the entire black business community to participate in a *CITI*works-type of economic development. At the same time, it removes the negative association of blacks with entitlement programs and more firmly documents how the entire community benefits from the results of transactions.

Chapter 4

The black experience has created a unique black market

"Success is not the result of spontaneous combustion. You must set yourself on fire."
— Fred Shero

*CITI*works and The 5% Solution Strategy

The black experience in America has created a black market that is unique to the black community. The secret to realizing the full potential of this market lies in tapping into five capabilities that are distinct to black life and culture. When these capabilities are developed into a *CITI*works plan and implemented through The 5% Solution Strategy, they have the ability to raise the profile of this distinct market and make it even more powerful. Those capabilities are:

- Direct black-to-black spending.
- Black businesses contracting with black businesses.
- Tourism created by black culture and heritage.
- Products and services blacks design specifically for the black market.
- Black involvement in the political process.

Let's look at each of these in more detail.

Capability No. 1: Direct black-to-black spending.

This is the primary market, and the thrust of The 5% Solution Strategy. It needs to be thought of in economic terms. The goal of The 5% Solution Strategy is to re-direct the spending habits of blacks from their dependence on majority white businesses to supporting black businesses. Statistics show that black people spend more than $113 billion annually. The idea is to increase the share of black spending power with black businesses.

This is where the black community can get creative in supporting black businesses. For example, I know of a small group of churches that came together to purchase their toothpaste from a particular business in their neighborhood. That simple strategy increased sales to the point that the business owner had to hire a part-time employee just to "take care of the toothpaste!" This is a perfect illustration of the *CITI*works example of supporting a black business because the business offers what black consumers want rather than simply buying from the business because the owner is black.

The entrepreneur who is seeking to grow his/her business with the black market must adapt to the customer tastes of their market. That may mean more professionalism, or sales courtesies. It could even mean more and better inventory. But it is gives the customer what the customer wants in order to generate repeat sales. It may also mean adapting to the black business culture if your business depends solely or largely on that market segment. For example, let me tell you about a business that through the years has morphed in various forms of the same business. This business has a sole employee, the owner, who I will call the "Sock Man"!

I noticed "Sock Man" selling socks, nothing but socks, out of the trunk of his car years ago. He was selling 60 pair for $10 all over the black community. Business was so good he started selling out of trailers. He had these permanent trailers with tents on the same corners where he had been selling out of the trunk of his car. He also started advertising his sales with a hand-drawn sign that offered customers the opportunity to "hook up" on socks. Business continued at such a pace that he decided to move the business into a retail store with professional signs. That didn't work out so well. Before long, he was back on the street corners with his trailers and tents. It appears that his customers didn't want to go into a retail store. They wanted to be "hooked' up out of his car trunk or a trailer. There is a uniqueness to some black consumers, particularly those who live within the more economically deprived inner-city areas that were Sock Man's market.

CITIworks and The 5% Solution Strategy

The lesson learned is that The 5% Solution Strategy is about creativity and innovation.

Capability No. 2: Black businesses contracting with black businesses.

This market is a simple re-directing of the expected outcome from transactions that will occur when government agencies and non-profits contract with black-owned businesses rather than white-owned businesses. It is all about the Black Dollar turnover! Black communities are already challenged by the fact that they do not spend enough with black businesses and various black organizations to create a dollar turn of at least 4-5 times. This is the reason for the development of The 5% Solution Strategy. It addresses the dollar turnover and the dollar "exit," dollars that leave the black community for the major banks, which are white owned, and major employers, which are white owned and based outside the black community.

Here is where corporate and government spending through minority vendor programs should continue. These programs should also use different metrics to measure outcomes to ensure that everyone can see the value of these special initiatives to the community. By contracting with black businesses, in more cases than not, the dollar gets a chance to go from the black business owner, to the black bank, to the black accountant, to the black church, to the black non-profit, and on and on.

Capability No. 3: Tourism created by black culture and heritage.

This is a market this is created through the attractiveness and uniqueness of the black cultural experience and black history as a source of knowledge and understanding of African-Americans. Tourism data shows that black culture and history hold a special interest for people from all parts of the globe.

Entrepreneurs constantly embrace the special markets that result from the creation of products or services that have been adapted from black style, fashion, entertainment and aspects of black culture. Creating tourism markets from the black experience in America doesn't always mean looking back into the pages of history. It can and does also mean marketing recent black lifestyle and economic contributions. As Darren Perkins, author of *"Business is War,"* says: "Use culture as a weapon. The African-American culture must be viewed as a brand with enormous economic potential. Millions of consumers want stuff that looks, tastes and sounds like us. We would be stupid not to fill this vacuum with our genuine, homegrown products and services. We need to create businesses that fill the world's hunger for our creative and intellectual properties. If we do not do this, you can believe other copycat non-black enterprises surely will."

The opportunity for creating a black tourism market should focus on creating job and business opportunities utilizing black businesses and institutions already in place. In most of our cities, black institutions have been abandoned or ignored. Tourism offers the opportunity to take the existing infrastructure and leverage it to create an entirely new business opportunity. For example, Dr. Michael Porter of Harvard University has long espoused the formation of inner-city business clusters to create a synergy that was not there before. Maybe your city doesn't have a large black business population, but there still could be enough black businesses to form a restaurant and entertainment district like Beale Street in Memphis, known for its rock and roll, gospel, R&B, jazz, and restaurants, or even a black version of San Francisco's China Town.

Think about what is unique about what black businesses are doing now in your town and how you can take advantage of those things through clustering and tourism to increase the amount of Black Dollars being spent, thus turned over, in your city. Tourism is your opportunity to attract visitors from your metro region, across the country as well as those from other countries. A tourism trail connected to your local school system would help children in your community understand the important role blacks have played in their city and, perhaps, give them an early education on future business doors that are there for them to open. Most importantly, tourism can create jobs that don't necessarily require a high education level or a long employment resume. In many cases, with tourism the greatest ingredient for success is an independent spirit and a passion to tell the story of the black experience.

Capability No. 4: Products and services blacks design specifically for the black market.

These markets are the obvious result of the ability of individuals and companies to develop a product or service that many in the black community find worthy. This type of business simply answers a need that may have a special appeal and is supported by black buying power within these special markets.

Many of today's best-known hip-hop and sports personalities are responding to market opportunities that are missing in the black community and that are attractive to the black consumer. These businesses often involve apparel, beverages, food, education, cars, healthcare, tobacco and travel. They create jobs and increase the standard of living for everyone involved.

Here are some strategies the would-be entrepreneur who wants to enter this market sector should consider:

- Create a product or service that has a niche identity or fulfills a niche need.
- It is often more profitable to create a new product or service and totally dominate the market than to sell products and services that are available from competitors.
- Because black businesses are naturally affiliated with the black community, the challenge will be to market the product or service so that the brand is recognized as distinct and specifically benefitting the black community.
- Develop a creative monopoly so that everybody who wants the product or service has to come to you.
- Don't follow the crowd; find the blank spots on the map.
- Study any relevant history about your product or service and integrate that into your marketing or business development.
- Study the competition as it develops.
- Realize that competition becomes a proxy for value.
- Don't let competition has trump value-creation or innovation.

Following these guidelines will require you to write a different type of business plan. Black business owners should think about developing their business to scale using black investment dollars or angel investors. A different kind of business plan in this case is one that clearly points out where the market is, how the business owner can gain market share or dominate the market, how he or she can minimize risk and how the business will produce ROI. The challenge, of course, is answering the question: "How do I move the needle?"

Capability No. 5: Black involvement in the political process.

Finally, blacks must change the political landscape to gain the influence to fully take advantage of the economic opportunities that are available to them. They must join in the political game and become involved all the way down to often-unnoticed races such as judgeships. Judgeships, arguably, have the possibility of touching a black business owner more than any other elected position. However, voters tend to pay them the least attention. Blacks need to form Political Action Committee (PACS) to gain the attention and the respect of politicians that can come from funding campaigns. We must educate politicians about economic and other issues that affect the black community that judges and politicians need to address to win the support of black business.

Countries like China, Japan, and Saudi Arabia have invested trillions of dollars in America, which gives them political power. African-American politicians, on the other hand, represent the agenda of the political party to which they belong, but not the African-American agenda. When you have economic power, you automatically have political power. This is straight forward truism. Think of the saying: He who pays the piper calls the tune. Let me give you an example involving the first black Mayor of Atlanta, Maynard Jackson (1938-2003).

Jackson, who served three terms as mayor of the South's largest city, is considered the father of black business development in America. He created a model for involving blacks in city contracts that required 35 percent of all city contracts to go to black-owned businesses. This became the base program across the country for involving black businesses in municipal contracts. Jackson's policy so infuriated the white business establishment that he had difficulty raising money to run for a second term. The black business community stepped to the plate and raised his entire budget! This is a perfect illustration of how political involvement by black businesses can support black economics for the masses, not just the individual. Remember, two-thirds of black businesses are made up black employees. When Jackson made sure black businesses were getting their fair share of Atlanta city contracts, he was ensuring jobs and income for black workers and their families.

The 5% Solution Strategy, the *CITI*works implementation tool, when coupled with redirected and outcome-articulated opportunities derived from black business support efforts such as Supplier Diversity and lending from banks and other sources, will create a visible Return on Investment that will support black business development in visible ways the entire black community can see and measure. The black community must be kept informed of these efforts at every opportunity through meetings as well as other forms of communication.

Turning the black market into a revenue stream

There are numerous other ways that black business owners can leverage the competitive advantage of the black experience in America to make the unique black market one of their revenue streams. These include:

- Providing exceptional customer service, including respect for the customer.
- Hiring black people.
- Being visible with the black community.
    - Provide knowledge and skills to black organizations, youth, etc.
    - Participate in the educational system (you and your employees).
    - Strive for continual customer improvement outcomes.
- Create or support a black business organization and lead the planning for its success and continuation.

- Give back to the black community 5 percent or more annually.
- Conduct at least 5 percent of your business-to-business spending with capable black businesses and organizations. (Keep in mind, though, that leading the battle doesn't mean not participating in the larger market!)

To be sure, black people face challenges in implementing the 5% Solution Strategy and solving our community deficit problems. These include:

- Seeking to be our own people by treating ourselves equally and shrugging off the plantation mentality (Post Traumatic Slavery Syndrome).
    - Stepping up to the plate and having our economics matter.
- Weeding from our minds the thinking that blacks should support black businesses just because they are black owned. Blacks should support black-owned business because they offer products and services that solve black consumer/business needs and wants.
    - When blacks fail to do business with each other they inadvertently surrender the black market and the advantages the black market provides black businesses.
- Continuing to grow supply chain purchasing efforts within corporations and governments.
    - We should collect and tabulate the economic data these efforts create and use the data to demonstrate exactly where employment is generated.

In all of these efforts, blacks should remember that the 5 percent spending goal is a minimum. It is not a ceiling. A recent survey conducted by the Atlanta business league revealed that more than 90 percent of those who are following The 5% Solution Strategy are spending more than 5 percent with black businesses and many are spending as much as 95 percent with fellow blacks.

Chapter 5

America's taboo subject ... race

"I have learned that success is to be measured not so much by the position that one has reached in life as by the obstacles overcome in trying to succeed."
  Booker T. Washington

Any issue related to race causes many communities to struggle with complex emotions and historical baggage. Perhaps that is why most communities do not establish black business development as one of their top economic development opportunities. Unfortunately, this added level of political racial matrix threatens to rob communities of what is a growing opportunity to regenerate American cities through the lens of black businesses. Even worse, American cities are facing this reality at a time when the opportunity for achievable black business development has never been better. To overcome the hurdles America's racist past presents and to make black business development an effective economic tool will require what every important community effort requires: strong leadership, effective planning, focus, and resources.

Another key to developing black businesses, according to Dr. Mel Gravely, managing director of the Institute for Entrepreneurial Thinking, is to make the effort important. Located in Cincinnati, the Institute provides leadership for minority entrepreneurs. To paraphrase Dr. Gravely: "If it is important it should look it. Bring the same approach used for other significant community commitments like convention center expansions, new sports venues and the re-development of historic neighborhoods. The blueprint for success is the same. Do the same planning. Involve top talent. Engage consultants to enhance community expertise. Invest the same type of resources. This approach rarely happens because in most communities black business growth is not important as an economic development tool. It is a defense against some social downside or a response to race-related pressure. Poor planning, weak talent, and limited resources will yield weak results. This outcome is happening everyday in minority business development initiatives around the country."

Second, any serious approach to instituting *CITI*works must involve black business on the "Top Line." "Top Line" means that the white business leaders must be willing to accept and treat black business owners as equals. Black business leaders and their involvement must be built into *CITI*works, not simply attached to it as a "bolt-on" that can be discarded later. Problem solving must be driven by the expected and lasting results of inner-city economic development, not by meeting a social concern through a short-term fix that goes away in time. In the case of The 5% Solution Strategy, problem-solving action steps must be repeated over and over to begin to see the results. The results come from black businesses employing black people and meeting their requirements for economic and cultural growth. Over time, the results will expand and grow and cause other aspects of the community to be more and more involved with problem solving for the entire city.

Perhaps most importantly, everyone must be honest about a subject that is taboo in American society: *race*. The simple truth is that the residents of most inner-city communities are black. In an attempt to treat everyone fairly, the term 'color blind" is being substituted for "black" when race is discussed. This is especially true in the policy-making arena. The term refers to an effort to treat black people fairly, which means treating them equally with whites. Unfortunately, racial equality is far from a reality. The only thing that may be true with this effort is what Tim Wise, an anti-racist essayist, author and educator, says in his book "*Color Blindness*:" "Color-conscious approaches show promise in fostering an appreciation of another group's positive societal contributions, as well as structural constraints and advantages."

One of the problems with color-blind policies as a business stimulus is that the policies often have the unintended consequence of further marginalizing people of color. This happens because governments steer money to large companies with inside connections on bidding and to construction companies with bad records on racial inclusion. The *CITI*works plan calls for stimulus efforts to be targeted toward communities where the population is disproportionately of color and poverty rates are at least 50 percent above the national average.

When contracts are not awarded in this manner, Wise suggests that a penalty should be imposed. "Bar companies found guilty of intentional racial discrimination from receiving government contracts, tax breaks, or direct subsidies fro a period of ten years. Impose a two-strike rule for the receipt of government contracts, tax breaks or subsidies for companies that are found guilty of discriminating, even unintentionally, by virtue of policies."

The Conundrum

A conundrum *CITI*works faces is getting people to buy from black business out of need, not to support the business just because the owner is black. I read recently that the "the way blacks think about black business has decimated the revenue base of black businesses." The culprit is support mentality. The results of a recent poll illustrate my point.

Question: When you buy a book from a black book store in your community, do you make the purchase to support the store or to buy a book?
Answer: 83 percent said they made the purchase to support the store.
Question: When you buy books from Barnes and Noble, do you make the purchase to support the store or to buy a book?
Answer: 96 percent said they made the purchase to buy the book.

The point is that when a person buys something from a business it is because the business has something they need or want. When a person makes a decision to support a business, they make a purchase that they do not need or want. In the latter case, they are trying to be a good person and support what most likely is a start-up black enterprise. In other words, black attitudes about black businesses are about support while black attitudes about other businesses are about simply about making a purchase.

*CITI*works and The 5% Solution Strategy propose that blacks develop a brand loyalty to black businesses for the things they need and use. Another premise of the model is that black entrepreneurs must overcome the barriers to non-customers. Those barriers are:

- Complacency regarding black consumers and their shopping habits.
- Fear of marketing / prospecting to non-customers.
- Lack of access to information.
- Lack of leadership skills.
- Fear of repeating bad experiences.
- Lack of education.
- Perceived affordability.
- Fulfilling customer satisfaction requirements.

The model also suggests three steps black business owners can take to expand their businesses. Those steps include:

1. Reconstructing market boundaries.
2. Focusing on the big picture, not just the most recent numbers.
3. Reaching beyond existing demand.

Understanding how the black community got to where it is today in America provides a platform from which to take these three steps. In Section Three, we take the next step: A call to action!

Section three

A call to action!
*CITI*works and The 5% Solution Strategy

*"We cannot solve our problems
with the same level of thinking that created them."*
Albert Einstein

Chapter 1

A 'Black Blueprint' to revitalize America's inner cities

"A good system shortens the road to the goal."
Orison Marden

It is a slow day in Southwest Atlanta. The rain is beating down, and the streets are deserted. Times are tough, and everybody is in debt and living on credit. On this particular day, a well-to-do tourist drives into the inner city and stops at a hotel. He lays a $100 note on the desk and tells the hotel owner he wants to inspect the rooms upstairs to pick one to spend the night. The owner gives him a set of keys, and the visitor heads up the stairs. As soon as he disappears from sight, the hotelier grabs the $100 note and runs next door to pay his debt to the caterer. The caterer immediately dashes down the street and pays the butcher the $100 he owes him. The butcher takes the $100 and flies down the street to repay his debt to the grocer. The grocer takes the $100 note and heads off to the farmer's co-op at the gas station to pay his outstanding bill. The operator of the farmers' co-op takes the $100 note and runs to the hotel to put down a deposit for a meeting room for the annual holiday party he hosts for the co-op members. The hotel proprietor, suspecting the visitor has had time to finish his inspections, quickly places the $100 note back on the counter. Sure enough, at that moment the traveler comes down the stairs, picks up the $100 note without any clue as to how it has been used, says the rooms are not satisfactory, puts the money back in his wallet, and heads to another part of town. Now, you noticed, no one produced anything! No one earned anything! However, the whole of Southwest Atlanta it seems is now out of debt and looking to the future with a lot more optimism than anyone had just a short while ago. And that is how the "Black Dollar" can turn over and is the basis for how The 5% Solution Strategy works in the inner city.

This story is hypothetical, but it contains many truths. It shows that the assets – black consumers, black businesses and black civic and business organizations – are already in place in America's inner cities to turn over the Black Dollar as many times as possible before that dollar leaves the inner city. It also shows how turning the dollar over multiple times in the black community creates vibrant economic activity within the community. Until now, however, inner city black residents and business owners have given little thought to how their spending choices impact their community.

My business partner, Henry Whitlow, created a "Black Blueprint," which the Hudson Strategic Group refined, that we believe will show the black community the importance of making conscious decisions about how they spend their money. We are convinced that by changing perceptions and changing thinking about spending so that purchases redirect the Black Dollar to black businesses we can launch a nationwide movement that will leverage the culture of mostly back inner cities. Our "Black Blueprint" harnesses black spending through an equation of blacks contracting and doing business with black businesses. We believe the sum of this equation will add up to activity that will, over time, stimulate and support black employment and the development of the black communities in which these businesses are located and that the activity will revive not only the inner city but the city as a whole.

Cooperative economics and mutual support

We are calling this "Black Blueprint" *CITI*works – Community Improvement Through Involvement. The concept for *CITI*works is simple. *CITI*works is a community development strategy that is based on the saying that *"when the black community works, the entire city works."* We believe that for *CITI*works to be successful, the black community must first see itself as a market worthy of being tapped and utilized for the development of black businesses as employers. To help the black community see itself this way, we developed a strategic action plan that is the underpinning for the concept and implementation of *CITI*works. This action plan calls on the entire ecosystem of a local community to engage in cooperative economics and mutual support to change individual economic outcomes so that they align with the collective goals of the larger community.

We are calling this implementation plan The 5% Solution Strategy. It calls on all of the assets of the black community – black citizens, black businesses and black institutions – to support black businesses by making and keeping three key commitments:

- Every person will increase their annual spending with black businesses by 5 percent over the previous year.
- Every black business will increase its spending with other black businesses by 5 percent.
- Every civic/social/philanthropic organization will increase its spending and contributions with the black community by 5 percent.

By adopting The 5% Solution Strategy, black people in all walks of life will create an economic structure of investing in their local communities through a conscious decision to spend "Black Dollars" with black businesses!

Black businesses employ people, even if only the owner, who in-turn spend their revenues and their salaries throughout the city. They also pay and collect taxes, both of which are important to the economic vitality of a healthy community because they provide revenue benefits. A perhaps less-tangible benefit is that The 5% Solution Strategy recognizes black businesses as an economic engine because the business owners provide civic leadership.

*CITI*works and The 5% Solution Strategy speak to a 'shared value" that demonstrates to everyone, no matter where they live, that black entrepreneurship is a benefit to the entire community, individually and collectively, and is not simply a benefit to the individual black entrepreneur. Implementing The 5% Solution Strategy will set the course to establish an economic inheritance that will help future generations of the black community to become self-sufficient if the plan is followed faithfully.

Three core principles

Successfully implementing The 5% Solution Strategy will require the inner-city community of each city to adopt a self-help doctrine based on three core principles:

1. Economic structure: Business and civic leaders will need to educate local communities about why individuals and the inner city community will benefit when blacks buy from black businesses.
2. Code of commitment: Black business owners will need to increase their involvement in their community through the educational system, philanthropic endeavors, and other civic activities – and they will need to stay committed.
3. Governance and organization: The community will need to develop a local organization to provide governance and support to ensure objectives are met.

*CITI*works and The 5% Solution Strategy address each of the principles in order to make them obtainable over time. *CITI*works and The 5% Solution Strategy are based on the understanding that consumers, black and non-black, have expectations from black businesses. These include at a minimum:

1. A professional business operation.
2. Products and services of value.
3. Customer knowledge.
4. Adequate finances.
5. Responsiveness.

The Return on the Investment in *CITI*works and The 5% Solution Strategy will include:

1. Increased opportunities for blacks to do business with blacks.
2. Increased marketing and awareness of black businesses.
3. An abundance of quality goods and services.
4. Job creation.
5. Support for the local community.
6. Self-discipline.

Give the community a voice in the plan

The key to developing an economic plan that brings value to the black community and its businesses is to create a plan that allows people in the community to see the benefit and want to participate. A way to encourage people to participate is to give them a voice in creating the plan. The best way to give them that voice is by holding collaborative meetings in which representatives of all the constituent groups can attend and participate.

Community representation at a minimum should have input from:

- Black businesses
- Black churches
- Black newspapers
- Black banks
- Youth
- Senior citizens
- Greek and other fraternal organizations
- Housing representatives
- Health field representatives
- Police and fire
- Local politicians
- Business and supplier development organizations

Why have this cross section? First, it is to educate the community about The 5% Solution Strategy and help the people who live there to understand its potential impact. Second, it is for buy-in. Third, because The 5% Solution Strategy is a long-term plan, it is to help the residents of the community understand how they will fit in over the long haul.

The plan must include several critical action steps. These include:

1. Setting goals. These goals must represent the long-range benefit the community is trying to

achieve through The 5% Solution Strategy. These goals should include such concerns as spending, who the initial beneficiaries will be, land use and development plans, and social impacts.
2. Creating value. The plan must explain how The 5% Solution Strategy will create value that will meet the needs of the community. For example, will the plan drive business sales, improve education, or create church ministries? These are just a few of the ways that The 5% Solution Strategy can create value. There are, of course, many others.
3. Leveraging resources. Plan leaders must determine the resources that exist in their community that are important to include in this effort. Here we are talking about business development organizations and other resource groups, labor support groups, and housing groups.
4. Honoring your heroes. Recognize the names and relationships of the many persons and groups involved at every opportunity. If things are printed, make sure the names are listed and pictures are included if possible. Acknowledge them as persons who provide input and decision making. Do not make the acknowledgements seem false and political but sincere and important. Do not create hierarchical lists by profession or some artificial standing. Instead, list names alphabetically or in some other straight forward manner. People love to see their names and to hear their input acknowledged!
5. Sharing information. Do not hoard it. Give it away at every possible opportunity! Give others a chance to further define the issues and come up with a response that is in keeping with the plan. Just stay in contact with them.
6. Closing gaps. Uncover what is necessary but missing that would help the plan become an effective strategy. Here we are requiring equity funds, different types of entrepreneurial training and education to come into play. In these cases, for example. the training may not be your ordinary "How to Start a Business" but may be "How to Read Your Environment for Success!"

Four ideas to achieve goals in the *CITI*works blueprint

Here are four unique ideas for cities to consider to close the racial equality gap and to achieve other goals when implementing the *CITI*works plan in your community:

1. Recruit and incentivize black businesses.
2. Replicate business models to spur business development.
3. Cluster businesses, especially businesses in the same industry sector.
4. Use all of the black business in the community, not just the large ones.

Let's look at each of these ideas in detail.

1. Recruit and incentivize black businesses

One of the challenges many cities face is, simply, a lack of black businesses, especially large black businesses. This is an especially unfortunate situation if the city's business base includes corporations. In cities where corporations make up the business base, there often are not enough black businesses to take advantage of corporate contract opportunities.

Where this is the case, the *CITI*works plan of action calls for city business and political leaders to market the city to black firms in other cities and to recruit those firms to relocate. There are black businesses in other cities that could be counted upon – if supported – to satisfy the needs of the city that is doing the recruiting. However, these black businesses will need something to relocate that is not normally offered to black businesses. That *something* is incentives.

CITIworks and The 5% Solution Strategy

Incentives can include such enticements as employee training, tax relief, free or discounted office or manufacturing space, and other contract support, including introductions to the contracting organizations and financial resources. It is worth stating again that these types of incentives must be driven by support from the political leadership as well as the business leadership.

Recruiting also provides an opportunity to take businesses to the "next level." In the *CITI*works model, the next level means an introduction to the important people and institutions that lead a city. It is the direct involvement of those organizations where important introductions and contacts are made. This is where deals are done and relationships are made, nurtured and sustained. The physical places where this happens are the Chamber of Commerce, the golf club, civic organizations, and the church!

2. The business replication model

Many new business owners find initial success but don't quite know how to either sustain that success or grow their business into a larger venture. This is where replication comes into play. If from the beginning the business will make a written record of its successful processes and document their function and how the company measures success, the business methods can be replicated.

Due to the role of technology in business development, it is now possible to create an exact operating model of a business. Using the franchise as an example, entrepreneurs from the beginning should write out a strategic plan to grow their business. With franchising, the franchise owner creates an overall strategic plan and operational management structure that establishes how the various functions of the enterprise work and how to problem-solve issues. Many marketplace tools for modeling and problem solving are available. Two for business owners to consider are the Malcolm Baldrige Collaborative Assessment and the Six Sigma program for problem solving.

3. Clustering

City leaders should ask themselves if there is a unique black industry in their city. If so, clustering those businesses can create an opportunity for the businesses to feed off of each other to generate revenue and at the same time create a possibility for tourism.

An example of a business cluster could be in the entertainment sector. In this case, a developer could bring together businesses such as film makers, studio owners, producers, technicians, writers, and other related service providers. Another example is the possibility of creating an African-American Village with great bistros and restaurants.

Clustering may pose challenges of various sorts, but the revenue possibilities make it worth the effort for business owners and civic leaders to consider the advantages clustering offers.

4. Use all of the black businesses in the community, not just the largest ones.

One of the easiest tools in the *CITI*works toolkit to implement, and one that is available to any community, is to include all of the businesses in the community in development plans. There is a tendency, however, to focus only on the largest businesses because those are the ones with the greatest employment. This is almost the exact opposite of the thinking of The 5% Solution Strategy. The 5% Solution Strategy is built upon street-level enterprise and mom and pop businesses. These are businesses that enable families to make a living. They also pay taxes, and most require a business license. These businesses range from what some might consider "hustling" to home-based businesses. In virtually every city, they form the basis of the business landscape of the inner city. More examples of these businesses include:

Barbers & beauticians	House keeping/maid services
Lawyers	Cook
Doctors and dentists	Personal services
Insurance sales	Recreational services – balloons
Dry cleaners	Taxi/jitney/driver
Gas stations	Horse and buggy
Tire shops	Dog walkers
Food franchises	Nurses (in home)
Nail shops	Bookkeeping/tax
Fruit vendors	Jewelry maker
Newspaper corner sales	Corner sales –fruits/Vegetables
Boot black	Hauling, property clean up
Auto repair	Babysitter – child care
Plumber	Auto brokerage
Roofers	Fence installation
Gutter cleaning	Handy man
Auto parking services	Notary
Auto cleanup	Pest control
Window washing	Trash and cardboard pick-up
Movers	Landscaping & Grass and lawn services
In-home sales: Avon, Tupperware, etc.	

A 5 percent growth in these businesses can greatly impact the turnover of the Black Dollar in the black community. These businesses are small and often self-employed ventures that require no special education or training. *CITI*works and The 5% Solution Strategy include them in re-development models because they represent many of the varied types of businesses that exist in the black community. Therefore, it is important that the voices of the owners of these businesses be heard as part of the solution to inner-city development efforts.

It is important to remember that while the business are often small, they are *businesses* that require a business license to operate and the business owners pay business taxes. The premise of the *CITI*works model is if that if you have a business license and pay taxes, then you are an important part of the business ecosystem of the black community. As such you contribute to the opportunity to provide turnover of the Black Dollar and have the opportunity to grow and develop the community through The 5% Solution Strategy. Because of their scale, these businesses are not always acknowledged when the subject of business development is discussed. Even though they may not conjure up the mental image of a typical business, they may represent self-employment at its finest – especially in the black community.

Chapter 2

The return on investment

"Why not go out on a limb? That's where the fruit is."
Will Rogers

Return on Investment (ROI) is a performance measure used to evaluate the efficiency of an investment. It provides a snapshot of profitability and historically has been used in a financial context. *CITI*works and The 5% Solution Strategy, which invest in communities and the people who live in them, take a different view of ROI. Rather than measuring ROI solely as the return on a monetary investment, *CITI*works and The 5% Solution Strategy primarily measure ROI in the benefits gained when individuals, companies, and governments invest resources in the inner city. In the case of *CITI*works and The 5% Solution Strategy, the investment is made through direct spending.

*CITI*works recognizes that when stakeholder groups invest in the inner city, they should expect and receive a return on their investment. Some of that return is an economic gain, to be sure. Much of it, however, is civic in nature. Some examples:
- Communities invest in infrastructure, education, and numerous services. They expect an ROI in employee benefits, payrolls, social services, and a variety of benefits from taxes.
- Investors put up their capital. They are looking for business opportunities from which they will make a profit on the money they invested.
- Business owners invest their personal capital and time. They want to be rewarded for their risk-taking by accruing wealth and having the opportunity to become an influence maker.
- Employees invest their time, talents, and emotions. They expect a secure work environment and a fair and steady salary.

While many inner-city residents have become conditioned not to expect any type of ROI from business or government investments, *CITI*works and The 5% Solution Strategy have developed the following formula for communities to measure ROI:
- Revenue = Dollar turnover, jobs, number of businesses created.
- Return = Business income, individual salaries, philanthropy.
- Assets = Black marketplace, quality businesses, business leadership.
- Profit = Safe community, improved schools, reduced crime, taxes collected.
- Investments = 5 percent increase in black spending, increased contracts, tax breaks, new sources of funds.

CITIworks is built on a ROI strategy in which success can be measured in a simple but truthful expression of benefits gained. Simply put, spending with black businesses produces jobs for black people and revenues for the business owners who, along with their employees, tend to spend the money they make in local businesses and financially support local institutions.

Dr. Boston, the Georgia Tech economics professor and president of Equant, described the ROI of investing in inner-city communities this way:
- Approximately 66 percent of the employees of a small business tend to reflect the race or ethnicity of the owner of the business.
- Approximately 44 percent of black businesses tend to locate in high-risk areas (usually assumed to be the mostly black inner-city or in poorer communities, which often are black).

Given these two facts, one could build the case that when blacks do business with black businesses their transactions will produce black jobs at a faster and more consistent rate than when they do business with business owners of other races or ethnicities. A third point made by other economists is that when blacks make philanthropic gifts they tend to make them to black causes or to causes sponsored by blacks.

This simple platform for *CITI*works and The 5% Solution Strategy is built not on conjecture or emotion but upon these three clear economic points. When conjecture and emotion are eliminated, the perception of some that black businesses are inferior by the nature of their black ownership should likewise be negated. From an economic perspective, the platform positions the black business community as having value and as a productive instrument for change. Creating value for black businesses enables them to become recognized as important to the life of the city. By moving from "a waste" to a marketplace necessity, the valued business:
- Becomes an asset worthy of investment.
- Assists in redeveloping and stabilizing inner-city communities.
- Helps cities develop a sustainable and first-mover competitive advantage.
- Positions black business owners to become a part of the leadership fabric of a city.

Debra Pankow, an extension family economics specialist and associate professor at South Dakota State University, says that "values are relatively permanent personal beliefs about what people regard as important, worthy, desirable or right. Values tend to reflect your upbringing and change very little without conscious effort throughout a lifetime. For example, some families and individuals hold their faith as a very high value; for others, education or a successful family business enterprise may be a value. Recognizing our values and understanding the values of other people with whom we closely interact is important."

Two types of value

There are two types of value:
Perceived – Alleged value.
Real – Authentic value.

Value from a community point of view is the ability to add something positive to the mix of individual and collective lives. Something positive in this case is the same as the business principle of ROI.

In CITIworks and The 5% Solution Strategy model, ROI is synonymous with value in several visible ways. Revenue equals dollar turnover, jobs produced and the number of businesses created. The community gains revenue from such sources as business income, individual salaries, and philanthropy. The community assets are the black marketplace, the quality of the businesses, and civic leadership from the business community. The community profits from a safe environment, improved schools, reduced crime, tax revenues, streetlights, street repair, recreational centers, libraries, parks, and pools. The community invests in their new opportunities by increasing black spending with black businesses, increasing contracts with black businesses, obtaining more tax breaks that support their concerns, and realizing new sources of funds.

Black businesses generate local dollar turnover, employment and community problem-solving abilities that support inner-city residents with additional possibilities for the resource allocations required to address community issues. Black businesses have always been an inexhaustible economic engine that provided these options. However, they have not always been recognized as such because of negative and incorrect perceptions about their size and numbers.

As a matter of perspective, the black business community makes the same economic contribution as it did during the days of segregation. In those days, black businesses provided goods or services that blacks required, requested and relished. This truism is based on the simple, but sad, historical reality that there was a time that blacks could not shop in the white marketplace because they were not welcome and often suffered some form of indignity if they attempted to do so.

Even though times have changed and black shoppers no longer face obstacles in buying goods and services from outside the black community, the economic impact of black purchasing power has not changed. By making enough purchases from black businesses, individuals hold the collective power to create jobs that will be filled from within their local community. The power of the black dollar remains the same from segregation days and, perhaps, has even grown stronger because black businesses can now benefit from spending by other community sources such as corporations and governments.

Knowing your community will help boost ROI

The entire community, black and white, should be exposed to the economic return on the investment that is being sought and generated and why this investment is important to the community. The community must also understand that the effort that is being undertaken is a campaign to obtain long-term results (ROI) rather than a one-time occasional effort for a short-lived benefit. The leadership in explaining the campaign and its objectives should come from the black business leadership.

One of the keys to obtaining the desired ROI lies in understanding the black community and what it has to offer. Black businesses, for instance, are no longer located on a single street or on streets in a certain part of town. These businesses frequently miss opportunities to grow because people in the black community simply do not know about them, which is a shame because there is a huge black customer base available to these businesses. Entrepreneurs have a greater ability now than before to build businesses that attract black customers because they can carry products or provide services that blacks need or want. Therefore they can attract the Black Dollar from a needs-based perspective rather than from people who will become clients simply to support a black person. One of the areas in which this is possible is in personal care products, which are extremely popular in the black community.

Another key to obtaining the desired ROI is that business owners must change their approach to doing business. They have the ability to out-maneuver the non-black competition because they know the market – the communities, the cities, black culture – better than anyone else. This is the black business owner's competitive advantage. What better advantage could a black entrepreneur ask for in starting a business in which he or she has a niche and about which he or she is passionate?

This competitive advantage can best be explained in the context of the whole city. What can the various segments of the black community – the clergy, nurses doctors and others involved in health and medicine, college fraternities and sororities, for example – do to become involved? *CITI*works gives black people the opportunity to change the perception of many that the inner city is a drain on resources and non-productive. *CITI*works creates the opportunity to develop strategies that create a community of recognizable value by developing strategies that turn non-productive assets into performing assets. To take advantage of these opportunities and maximize ROI for all stakeholders, black businesses need to untie their hands by advertising in black newspapers, magazines, and in other black media to establish brand recognition so that people looking for black businesses will know about them.

Chapter 3

*CITI*works is the inexhaustible economic engine of the inner city

*"Write the vision and make it plain
so that ALL who read it can run with it."*
Habakkuk 2:2

*CITI*works and The 5% Solution Strategy

How fast does *CITI*works begin to work? you might ask. Here's the answer: *CITI*works begins working the moment the black community begins to see itself as a market worthy of being tapped to develop black businesses as employers. When this realization sets in, *CITI*works becomes a toolkit that leverages the assets of the community to produce measurable value through the concept and implementation of The 5% Solution Strategy, the spending model in which blacks spend an additional 5 percent, year-over-year, with black businesses and organizations. Because the return on investment has a profound impact that is felt beyond the black community, the opportunities that *CITI*works makes possible can be best understood in the saying *"when the black community works, the entire city works."*

Why do we call this concept *CITI*works? To answer this question, remember what *CITI*works means: *Community Improvement Through Involvement*. Communities need strong local business leaders to champion opportunities to overcome local economic conditions. Likewise, the enterprise base of the black business community needs a planning framework that has as its priority retaining and growing sustainable black businesses. We call this model *CITI*works because it recognizes that the assets to address these concerns in a straightforward way are already in place in the form of inner-city black consumers, black businesses and black organizations.

When properly utilized, these assets will produce an economic return that will lead to resurgence not just of the inner city but of the entire city. In short, the *CITI*works self-help strategy of using black businesses as delivery partners because of their long-term involvement in the inner city and their commitment to the black community will work for everyone. Sadly, though, past efforts to support black businesses and the results of those efforts – creation of jobs, wealth, community development – have not been given the recognition they deserve.

*CITI*works accomplishes its goals in five primary ways. *CITI*works:

- Ties together various elements of black and minority business development – such as spending, financial assistance and personal spending – and converts these activities into economic outcomes of jobs, taxes, and improved social conditions.
- Redirects current and future resources to meet specific goals set by local communities.
- Recognizes that the fastest way for the black community to gain economic benefits is by developing and growing the assets that are already there.
- Creates profitable business opportunities.
- Helps black businesses attract a larger share of dollars already being spent.

By now, you are probably beginning to think about your own community and wondering how *CITI*works can lead to a resurgence of the black enclaves in your city or town. Perhaps you've even begun to ask yourself some thought-provoking questions about black businesses in the town, city and state where you live.

For *CITI*works and The 5% Solution Strategy to effectively address economic concerns and make corrections, civic and business leaders in each city that adopts the model should ask themselves the following questions about their own community:

1. Are we marginalizing black businesses when we recruit non-black businesses and ask them to relocate?
2. How can black businesses more effectively participate in and benefit from the regional business community?
3. Are black businesses major employers?
4. What are our city's or town's economic and cultural goals for the next five years and what role can black businesses play?
5. Do we have a five-year economic plan to award contracts to black and disadvantaged businesses or to engage their services in other ways?
6. Why did the minority quota process fail? Can or should the process be reinstalled or redesigned?
7. Do black businesses receive unfair advantages in our local marketplace?
8. How can black businesses be represented in discussions about regional growth and development? Or, are black businesses in our community "out-of-sight and out-of-mind."
9. What are the benefits of supporting local black business development and growth?
10. How can politically mobilizing the black business community gain equal opportunity over time?
11. Have we given enough thought to the what, when, where, why, and how of the economic benefits of black businesses?
12. What are the benefits of black business leaders becoming partners at the table of economic growth and development?
13. How can black businesses enhance the ability of our local government to serve constituents?
14. What is the value of minority business programs?

*CITI*works is about black entrepreneurship. However, the *CITI*works model can be applied to any small business community whether it is defined by race, ethnicity, or some other parameter. In application to any group and over time, *CITI*works addresses other systemic community problems. As an example, in its application to the inner-city black community and the inevitable racial overtones, *CITI*works also addresses relationship gaps between blacks and whites in areas such as education, employment, and income level.

The benefits of the *CITI*works model to entrepreneurship have far-reaching implications for community well-being, including clearing pathways to social and professional mobility, wealth creation and political power. Self-employment, a natural component of entrepreneurship, has become an integral part of the policies designed to improve the well being of groups with low educational attainment and income rates. For the most part, the current types of black businesses reflect the typically low educational level of the black community in which the business operates. As such, black businesses are a reflection of the community in which they reside.

Researchers (Fairchild, 2008) have raised the question of how socio-economic status and segregation affect black entrepreneurship. Their findings show that the clustering of a black population has a positive effect on the levels of entrepreneurship for communities with low education rates, while cross-racial interactions and integration have a particularly positive impact on black entrepreneurs who have a college education. At the same time, other researchers (Cutler and Glaeser, 1997) have found that exposure to positive role models, which is defined as anyone who has attended college regardless of whether they earned a degree, may have a positive impact on the socio-economic outcomes of members of a segregated community. They also found that blacks have more exposure to positive role models in cities with less residential segregation. Gentrification – the process by which the middle class, defined as relatively educated, and (usually) majority white, moves into an economically depressed, typically black, neighborhood – creates economic and housing improvements. As such, gentrification provides a unique opportunity to examine this hypothesis and to measure whether entrepreneurs and business owners within a community have been able to benefit from cross-racial interactions.

Understanding the black business opportunity!

Understanding of the history of the black business community and how it got to where it is today, as discussed in Section 3, is essential in understanding the opportunity that gentrification presents. When gentrification is understood in the perspective of how black people are an "overcoming people," it becomes easier to understand how the small black business owner has overcome the many battles inherent not only in entrepreneurship but against the historical backdrop of the Civil Rights movement. The progress of black business in America has been achieved through access to educational opportunities that didn't exist for previous generations of blacks, the aid of laws and regulations that supported black business development, a base of experience gained by previous generations of black business owners, and changes in racial attitudes in general. The result of these developments is a white community that has become increasingly more acceptable of the success of black businesses.

These hard-won changes have brought about black business persons who are better prepared to create larger and more sophisticated businesses than the pioneering black entrepreneurs who came before them. This new generation of black businesses has the capacity to endure because they are being managed by entrepreneurs who better understand business principles and thus are better equipped to do bigger deals than, in most cases, was previously realistic.

This latest generation of black business owners has begun to ascend from start-up models to larger-scale businesses. As beneficiaries of the foundation laid by their predecessors, they have the maturity to provide the type of civic leadership that is required to support and sustain all great cities. It is not important whether their business is located in the inner city or the suburbs. What is important is that their business will still resemble them in the racial makeup of the people they employ.

Businesses need the community as much as the community needs the businesses. Businesses look to communities for demand for their products and services as well as a supportive environment. Communities look to businesses for jobs and the opportunity to create wealth for their residents.

Black businesses as inner-city anchors

Despite their relative small size, inner-city black businesses have at their fingertips – next door, down the street, around the corner – a diverse under-employed workforce and advantageous locations. These realities provide inner city black businesses with sustainable competitive advantages that present them with the clear potential to become community anchors that will be an asset to inner-city enclaves as well as to entire cities. According to the Initiative for the Competitive Inner City, there are "seven capacities in which anchors typically interact with their communities." They are:

1. A provider of products or services.
2. A developer of real estate.
3. A purchaser.
4. An employer.
5. A workforce developer.
6. A cluster anchor.
7. A community infrastructure builder.

Black businesses historically have been inner-city anchors, perhaps not in the traditional sense of micro-economics, but within the practical sense of an inner-city operation. During tough times, many inner-city black businesses remain economically strong, even when businesses outside the inner city are failing. Yet, the relative economic health of black businesses, combined with the fact that they can be seen as operating or functioning under a different business model, often makes them a target of resentment. Black businesses, however, often are not seen at all. Rarely are they seen as integral to the local economic system or as an important asset. Why has the non-black community failed to recognize the contributions of black businesses to the overall American socio-economic structure? I believe it is because the business models of black businesses reflect the separate, unique and distinct black experience in America.

In spite of the uniqueness of the black experience and the makeup of the black business model, the guiding premise of *CITI*works is that all segments of a community contribute to a city's success. As such, *CITI*works creates value that makes the city worthy of investment by others by:
  • Assisting in the redevelopment and stabilization of inner-city communities.
  • Helping a city develop a sustainable and first-mover competitive advantage.
  • Helping black businesses owners become part of a city's leadership team.
  • Supporting politicians and community concerns.

Another key premise of the *CITI*works model is that it creates jobs because of enterprises and organizations that exist in the inner city, not in spite of them. As these jobs are created and the community invests in the businesses through the additional spending of The 5% Solution Strategy, the resulting increase in revenue will allow black enterprises to scale up. This in turn will allow the business owners to hire additional employees to meet the increase in demand for the goods and services offered by the businesses. Increasing employment in the black community will have a positive across-the-board impact on the inner city, the city as a whole and the region around the city. The hiring potential of black employers is critical to the micro-economic health of communities and the macro-economic health of the country. That's because there is a gap between the types of skills needed by the businesses blacks will open and skills required by large corporations or non-profits. This gap has created a pool of people, many of whom are black, who are looking for jobs that black businesses create. This example is typical of how *CITI*works and

The 5% Solution Strategy address many of the skill and efficiency gaps often associated with economic development of minority communities.

*CITI*works reduces the need for entitlements

*CITI*works produces another economic benefit that is a direct result of creating jobs. The wages from these jobs and the turnover of dollars in the inner city reduce the constant cry for external government funds, also known rightly or wrongly as entitlement programs, to support minorities. Further, *CITI*works underpins the community in numerous other ways critical to economic stability. These include:
1. Employment benefits: In addition to providing wages and insurance benefits, new businesses and new jobs will result in retirement plans for owners and employees.
2. Shareholder value: The community will realize dividends such as stability and opportunities for growth.
3. Financial stability: Repayment of loan and credit obligations.
4. Government revenue: Collection and payment of taxes.
5. Community investment: Supporting local infrastructure, health, education, and social organizations.
6. Providing government financial assistance: Black businesses do not receive significant financial aid from local governments other than contractual.
7. Local recruitment: Hiring employees locally and providing contracts to local and regional businesses.
8. Regional growth: Business activities in the inner city and larger black communities will help other economic sectors of the metro area grow.

Statistics show that black businesses are located in under-served communities but account for a growing percentage of U.S. jobs and the country's demand for goods and services. *CITI*works recognizes the "powerful legacy" of black people, black businesses and black communities. The need for them to rise to their competitive capacity is critical, not only for the future of blacks as a race but to the nation as a whole and the cities that are its lifeblood.

Inner-city black enclaves have other competitive advantages rooted in the black culture. These include:
- Spending power. Black consumer spending has reached $913 billion annually. It was expected to hit $1.3 trillion in 2013. This is a huge market and is the basis for the 5% Solution Strategy!
- Black creativity. People emulate the Afro-centric culture, its products and its ideas. Think hip-hop, clothes and accessories. Businesses that fill the world's hunger for black creative and intellectual property are creating niche opportunities and forcing the mainstream to come to the black community for business and cultural leadership as well as goods and services.
- Tourism. Mainstream guidebooks and tourist agencies often ignore Afro-centric culture and history. Some cities have taken advantage of the rich history their cities created during the Civil Rights strife of the late 1960s and '70s or the successes of their communities or historically important black leaders. However, there are many more tourism opportunities that cities can capitalize on to help visitors as well as local students

recognize the legacy of black contributions and successes to America's history. For example: the black business districts of Atlanta or of Richmond could be better cataloged and preserved and featured by city marketing departments, chambers of commerce and tourist agencies as valuable assets of local communities.

Problem Solver – *CITI*works!

To achieve its goals of black and other inner-city businesses being seen as assets and contributors to community growth and stability, and for black business owners to become recognized as leaders in city government, *CITI*works requires that we must change the paradigm. In doing that, *CITI*works says we must change the language about black business to an economic conversation that includes jobs, poverty reduction, and economic development. A part of that new paradigm is allowing the black and inner-city community to define success and stop allowing others to define it for them. This is an important step because the definer usually will define things in their favor, not someone else's! Therefore, *CITI*works requires that local communities become their own advocate!

*CITI*works also encourages value innovation! This term can be best explained as developing those opportunities that lie outside the envelope, which is to say not just the opportunities that are obvious. In the case of inner-city economic development, *CITI*works encourages local tax incentives and similar subsidies to support community businesses. The *CITI*works model even encourages cities to recruit black businesses from other cities in other states.

In a macro sense, *CITI*works weaves what until now have been various disjointed efforts into a unique and forward thinking fabric to support black and minority businesses. Previously, programs and toolsets to aid black and minority businesses have not had a single lens through which to view their combined contributions to the community. These programs have not only faced their own struggles to survive, they have not been appreciated for the valuable contributions they have made to communities. *CITI*works corrects these problems. It provides that much-needed single lens to view these programs both for the ways they benefit a single minority business or a group of minority businesses as well as for their aggregate contributions to improving the socio-economics of entire communities.

It is important to also understand that while the successes of previous support programs may be under-appreciated, they indeed benefitted black communities both as individual agencies, as laws and as a minority support movement. Consider, for example, where black and minority businesses and communities would be without the Small Business Administration's 8 (a) program, corporate supplier diversity initiatives, the federal government's Equal Opportunity acts, or community investment by banks. These efforts have been supported by laws or regulations such as Public law 95-507 (enacted in 1978, made federal procurement more readily accessible to all small businesses); Public Law 95-89 (enacted in 1977, increased loan authorizations and surety bond guarantee authority to minority businesses); Public Law 99-661 (enacted in 1986, required affirmative efforts by all government contractors towards a three-year goal of 5 percent minority (disadvantaged) business participation in Department of Defense procurement); coupled with affirmative action such as Title VII of the Civil Rights Act of 1964 (protects individuals against employment discrimination on the bases of race and color, as well as national origin, sex, and religion) and Title 41 (provides equal opportunity for minority contractors in highway projects); and Executive Order 11625 (issued in 1971, designated blacks, Puerto-Ricans, Spanish-speaking Americans, American Indians, Eskimos, and Aleuts as persons who are socially or economically disadvantaged and thus eligible for MBDA assistance from the Minority Business Development Agency).

When viewed as an entire developmental effort designed to produce jobs and create economic benefits, these regulations and laws have clearly been successful. It doesn't matter that some people view them as ineffective and others see them as entitlements, they have none-the-less significantly contributed to the development and support of black and minority businesses. However, neither their economic impact nor the effect they have had on alleviating the scourge of discrimination have been definitively measured. Interestingly, Public Law 99-661 has a 5 percent participation goal for procurement of Defense Department contracts. *CITI*works demonstrates how The 5% Strategy Solution would increase spending by blacks and others with black businesses and would begin creating new jobs within one year, with more than 66 percent of those jobs going to black people!

Cluster ecosystems are untapped opportunities

Another term that *CITI*works embraces is "shared value." Don't think of this as a social responsibility. It is an economic concept that offers a new path to economic success. The concept of shared value recognizes that black businesses and their communities are inextricably bound together. Shared value policies and operating practices enhance the competitiveness of a company while simultaneously advancing the economic and social conditions in the communities in which it operates.

The Initiative for a Competitive Inner City (ICIC) has studied inner-city economies in 100 U.S. metropolitan areas since 1994 and conducted on-the-ground consulting engagements in 20 inner cities. The study identified a set of strategies and best practices for growing inner-city economies and creating jobs. Among these is a cluster-led approach that identifies market opportunities and focuses on efforts to attract businesses to communities and to retain them once they are established.

A cluster is a group of companies and industries located in a geographic area. Clusters function as an economic "ecosystem" because their activities are interrelated. Transportation and Logistics is an example of an industry cluster. Likewise, Entertainment, Education, Business Services and Healthcare are also clusters. *CITI*works encourages cluster-led economic development because this approach has the potential to be a successful development strategy around which inner-city black businesses can rally.

*CITI*works believes that there is the potential for cluster-type economic development "ecosystems" in many communities and encourages city leaders to look at what those opportunities might be. Atlanta, for example, is heavily invested in entertainment/hip hop, with many successful, filmmakers, producers, writers, artists, studios for various segments of the industry, and musicians operating in the city and region.

These elements could easily be developed into an entertainment community in one major location. Uniting these various but related businesses would create a synergistic community and a tourist attraction as well. Black developers could lead this effort and fund it with black capital from black banks and black investors plus the financial support from within the black entertainment industry. Black communities also have great potential for affinity type of community clusters that could include an Africa Town modeled after a China Town.

A street level view of job creation

In today's world, it is common for local government leaders to appeal to the black community to support large projects that need public support. The appeals often come in the form of inducements such as jobs and sub-contracting opportunities for black and minority businesses. Government officials may also dangle the carrot of job training as an incentive for community support. This is a perfect example of "stakeholder fatigue." Black communities have heard this story before. They also know how the story ends. Typically, it's with few concrete results, especially in the form of anything tangible for the community to build on when the project was completed. Therefore, black communities have become "fatigued" by these types of offers and in most cases have finally stopped believing the promised outcomes.

What black communities need when governments seek their endorsement for these types of projects are specific examples that illustrate how the community will become a true beneficiary. They need to see themselves as the person getting the job rather than a general life-will-be-better promise. This is where *CITI*works brings proposed projects down to street level. By requiring black contractors be involved in the project – and with the knowledge that black firms hire more blacks than any other racial or ethnic group, especially those with less-than-ideal qualifications – community members will see themselves as truly involved and directly benefitting from the project. Over time, this process will help virtually everyone in the community know someone who got a job as a result of the *CITI*works approach.

Also, the chance of the person keeping the job after the project is completed is greater with a local employer than it would be with a non-local employer. When the project is finished and the employer's project leaders return to the company's distant city, what are the chances the company will offer the local employees a job in that city? What are the chances that even if they are offered a job, the employee could relocate? Slim to none in either case! The local black contractor is within the worker's travel budget and, provided there are continued employment openings, can keep the person(s) employed. The value of this situation to residents of the local black communities is that they have the possibility of being employed over a long length of time versus only being employed for the length of a particular contract. Plus, the combination of local black businesses and local black employees offers even more opportunities for turning the dollar over within the community, thus initiating and sustaining The 5% Solution Strategy.

Residents of a community understand economic and other benefits of new businesses and job creation in simple terms. Workers view their benefits in salaries. Business owners view their benefits as the income their small business may generate. The community sees its benefits as better schools, lower crime rates, an increase in taxes created and collected and improvements in infrastructure that the new tax revenues support. Local business owners are also looking for an

ROI on increased spending. They will measure their ROI in more contracts and business opportunities from the larger community along with tax breaks and, hopefully, new sources of funding to grow their businesses. This is why it is important to change the language around community development from the language of business or government that most people do not understand to the more easily understood simple language of The 5% Solution Strategy.

Importantly, The 5% Solution Strategy does not blame racism for problems in the black community. Instead, it simply recognizes racism as a condition that must continually be dealt with because of its institutional nature. In the language of *CITI*works and The 5% Solution Strategy, the reference to racism as institutional refers to patterns of discrimination affecting racialized groups. In this case, one group (white people) benefit from these patterns and another group (blacks) suffer from these patterns. Discrimination, refers to patterns of oppressive behavior – which can occur without prejudice. In the *CITI*works and The 5% Solution Strategy, actions that suppress oppression are not discriminatory, for this would make liberation the equivalent of slavery.

*CITI*works and The 5% Solution Strategy emphasize that institutional patterns do not depend on purposeful action (or positive racist motive), what some people mistakenly call "intentional." Rather, these patterns are determined/identified by results, by biases inherent in their operation. As feminist scholar Jo Freeman puts it: "Institutional discrimination is built into the normal working relationships of institutions, its perpetuation requires only that people continue 'business as usual.' Its eradication requires much more than good will; it requires active review of the assumptions and practices by which the institution operates, and revision of those found to have discriminatory results."

The patterns of institutional racism clearly run in the direction of white privilege and black disadvantage. Whites enjoy better and higher paying jobs, better educational outcomes, lower rates of unemployment, longer lives, fewer diseases and illnesses, lower rates of infant mortality, lower rates of poverty, lower rates of incarceration, greater home ownership, better homes, and so forth. All of these are empirically rooted in patterns of institutional discrimination. Failure to act to overthrow these patterns is a manifestation of racism.

Despite the historical record, however, blacks need to stop blaming America's racist past for the conditions that exist in the black community today. Even though racism produced the current conditions, the historical record is what it is and it can't be changed. Going forward, *CITI*works and The 5% Solutions Strategy offer each inner-city community in America a guideline to reach its full potential for business success and social enjoyment. In adopting this approach, each community is encouraged to develop a 2-10-year outlook.

"When the black community works, the entire city works"

*CITI*works and The 5% Solution Strategy can easily be combined with other initiatives. Think of how *CITI*works and The 5% Solution Strategy could work in your own city as you consider these general examples of the flexible nature of this new approach to revitalizing America's cities.

- ***CITI*works** serves as the mission and business model for inner city community development and has the express purpose of improving community economic outcomes.

- ***CITI*works** attempts to acknowledge and align strategies to support business development, job creation and other economic benefits.

- ***CITI*works** provides an economic flow chart to grow the economy of any city or community. The flow goes like this: The city needs to grow its businesses. To grow its businesses, it needs to improve their quality. To improve their quality, it needs to increase the skill of the workforce. Improving the skill of the workforce will help lead to acceptance and success of the business. Acceptance and success of the business will help grow the local economy.

- ***CITI*works** brings together a cross section of participants in the inner city and allows them to develop a strategy to use black businesses to create sustainable growth based on the unique nature of each individual city.

- ***CITI*works** encourages purchasing by non-locals through efforts that stimulate minimum push back, such as tourism.

- ***CITI*works** produces unexpected benefits for the inner city and entire city.

- ***CITI*works** changes the language and the game!

- ***CITI*works** produces measurable results.

- ***CITI*works** provides a platform for lack business owners to have a seat at the table of civic leadership, not only of the inner city but of the entire city.

- ***CITI*works** turns over the dollar within the black business community, which facilitates community development.

- ***CITI*works** is about the unrecognized ability of black businesses to create an economic advantage for cities and states.

- ***CITI*works** is a competitive advantage because most black business owners know the market, live, work or shop within it, have the overall business intelligence to participate in it and are familiar with many of the people, businesses and politicians located there.

- ***CITI*works** provides a mandate for the black business employer to improve life in America's inner cities.

- ***CITI*works** is predicated upon the existence of viable black businesses and is a statement of productivity and hope for the black community.

Chapter 4

Creating black business value with The 5% Solution Strategy

"You have to cut the garment to fit the cloth."
John Cox

The biggest challenge to creating value for black businesses with The 5% Solution Strategy is overcoming negative perceptions about black businesses and the inner city. Perhaps the second biggest challenge is a tendency to compare one thing to another. Who has the biggest? Who has the best? For The 5% Solution Strategy to be a successful economic tool, two critical difference-makers must happen before we begin implementing the strategy. First, before we can change inner cities across the country, we must accept them as they are, not as we might want them to be. Second, we must also understand that the "as they are" values are unique to each inner-city community. The inner-city black community in Atlanta is different from the inner city in Washington, D.C., which is different from the inner city in New York, which is different from the inner city in Detroit, which is different from the inner city in Los Angeles. While some issues, no doubt, are similar, most are unique to each inner city because of who lives there and who those residents want to live there.

The 5% Solution Strategy assumes that each inner-city community has value and that each community has its own value proposition. Therefore, people, jobs, and experiences must be valued for their effect upon their particular community, not upon an artificial, cookie-cutter, one-size-fits-all standard that economists or urban community planners might develop as a short-cut solution. The 5% Solution Strategy realizes that revitalizing America's inner cities is different from selling hamburgers or fried chicken – creating a franchise community isn't the way to go.

The cookie-cutter analogy applies to the larger community as well. Business structures in the black community do not always look like business structures in the suburban white community. Inner-city black businesses tend to be sole proprietorships and friendship-developed partnerships rather than corporations and limited liability corporations (LLC's). Nevertheless, the same economic, sales-driven, employment-based actions are going on within the inner-city black community as in the suburbs. Additionally, black businesses often do not need highly skilled employees. Because suits are not always required, black businesses frequently look the same. However, as these businesses grow in sophistication and scale, they will employ persons with higher skill levels.

The premise that each community must chart its own course so it can reach the specific outcomes needed by that community is based on the recognition that economic activity is going on inside the community. This is true even if people outside that community are unaware of it or ignore it as though it is almost non-existent. People in the inner city do respond to new markets and they do exchange money. They hire people and they supervise them. Because the methodologies are sometimes not the same as in the suburbs, the vibrant economic commerce of the inner city is often not appreciated by people who do not live there. However, the reality is that economic activity does exist, and the inner-city economy does manage to blossom no matter the country's general economic conditions.

There's money in the inner city

Want evidence that money is circulating within the black community? Just look down the street, or around the corner, or on the next block. You'll likely see large operations such as Wal-

Mart, Max's, Titlemax, Family Dollar, The Dollar Store, CITI Trends, and Walgreens. In fact, Wal-Mart is a trend-setter in developing a new and different business model specifically for the inner city. Businesses such as the ones mentioned here that locate in the inner-city adapt their processes to match the realities of the community in order to gain the sales and achieve the economic outcomes they seek for their shareholders. They have figured out how to deal with problems such as shoplifting, loitering, and disengaged employees that are typically associated with lower-income, inner-city residents.

Another example of money circulating in the inner city is the re-emergence of the "gas station." There was a period in which very few oil companies would open a gas station in an inner-city community. However, "gas stations" are now popping up in inner cities across the country. These are the same types of gas stations that we see on thoroughfares across America, which is a different business model, of course, than people of a certain age remember. The days when an attendant would pump a driver's gas and wipe their windshield are long gone! The new model is a food mart with several pumps. Food marts and black spending are compatible because of the absence of traditional grocery stores in inner cities. The marts specialize in the snacks and other quick-food items that are consistent with the historically poor diets of inner-city residents. The large box stores and marts also meet other lifestyle needs of inner-city residents, such as lay-away services, check cashing, and wire transfers. Even in middle-class black areas large businesses are beginning to expand product lines and services to attract the Black Dollar. This trend includes sales of franchises to blacks, which in turn creates more black employers and black jobs.

The 5% Solution Strategy assumes that black people understand the benefits of turning the Black Dollar over in the black community, have an affinity for other black business owners and will do business with other black people. Unfortunately, that assumption is sill seeking validity in today's mass-market world. Black people, particularly the young, no longer feel a sense of responsibility to support black businesses even if their parents and senior members of the community hold this obligation in high regard. Instead of feeling an obligation to others of their own race, the obligation today seems to be to self, perhaps best expressed in the popular acronym, WIIFM (What's In It For *ME*?).

Change the game and the language

The social injustices of the past have left scars that continue to pose a serious impediment to black businesses. This is something that black business owners must reckon with in an open and forthright way. Glossing over the past and trying to recognize past wrongs for anything other than what they were will not change the reality that people in black communities have constantly experienced broken promises. These broken promises have lead to mistrust and even inaction among black people. Further complicating the problem, new answers to questions addressing issues in the black community have been couched in the same language as solutions that have been proposed in the past. The result is that the black community hasn't seen new policies that offer realistic hope for a better lifestyle. What they have seen are broken promises that were offered again in "warmed-over" language. *CITI*works and The 5% Solution Strategy seek to *change the game and the language.* The old language included terms such as discrimination, set-aside, racism, and community relations. The new language includes terms such as specific local jobs created, taxes paid, performance management, and statistical outcomes.

The negative impact of the scars of social injustice and the attempts to clarify new strategies in old language that didn't lead to promised results may be the biggest malaise that *CITI*works and The 5% Solution Strategy face in helping the black inner city lead the revival of American cities. Here's why. Citizens, civic, and other groups are increasingly holding organizations and governments accountable for delivering on their promises. They are carefully measuring what is delivered against what was promised. It is becoming evident that unless organizations help their stakeholders achieve their individual or collective goals, the stakeholders will lose faith in government and other civic processes. When that happens, their natural tendency is to say '*I've heard that before. It didn't work then, and it ain't going to work now.*' When people think in this manner, they become jaded, cynical, lose their objectivity and emotionally drop out of efforts to improve their community even though they still live there. When people in a community drop out, everyone – including people in the larger community, whether that community is a city, a metro region, or even the entire nation – loses.

Stakeholder fatigue and misconceptions about black businesses

Two of the underlying forces that cause blacks to lose hope and drop out are stakeholder fatigue and widely held misconceptions about black businesses. Continuous revisions in a community's mission are a major contributing factor to stakeholder fatigue. This phenomena occurs when there are repeated changes in administration, philosophy, or other marketplace concerns. It isn't that change isn't appropriate. Change should, however, always be aligned with stakeholder and contributor expectations. To accomplish this, stakeholders should be continuously involved in the planning and implementation process. Involving stakeholders is the best way to ensure that governments and organizations live up to their ability to meet shareholder expectations and to sustain these entities during the long haul.

When the new strategies and control techniques of *CITI*works and The 5% Solution Strategy are applied, community problems can be eliminated and eventually prevented. The key to achieving success is for communities to develop a sustainable objective strategy and implementation methodology that is aligned with those of its various stakeholders and contributors. This means that community leaders must agree on what changes are needed, manage the implementation of those changes, develop ways to measure the effectiveness of the changes, monitor the system, and make the necessary tweaks that will inevitably be needed to ensure the changes continue to work as intended. They also must address stakeholder fatigue by creating a new game plan that attracts and retains stakeholders. It is perfectly fine to write this game plan from a script that has been used in the past, but it must be supplemented with new scoring plays (i.e. habits) and modified as needed to meet changing circumstances without adversely affecting its mission or reason for existence.

Misconceptions about the contributions and value that black businesses bring to the black as well as the larger community have also had a serious detrimental effect on the black community. While it is true that black businesses are smaller in size than many other types of businesses, they none-the-less provide a constant source of economic benefit within the black community. As black businesses continue to grow, their economic impact will also grow! It is only a perception, and a wrong one, that black businesses don't bring economic value. The facts are that black businesses do bring value. Better yet, they have the potential to bring much more value through The 5% Solution Strategy.

Another misconception is that black businesses offer substandard products and services that don't measure up to those of white businesses. Unfortunately, people have come to believe this myth and tend to apply it to every black small business when it may only be a problem of a few. Even so, it has created a false pain of discomfort about black businesses that has led to an expectation of disappointment. When people experience – or perceive – disappointments in their relationships, they become jaded and no longer objective about why things have happened. These emotions often lead to negative feelings. The natural reaction is for them to take actions that relieve their pain. In this case, people lose the enthusiasm to participate and not purchase goods and services from black businesses.

Weeding out the capable businesses and organizations from those that are not capable is a major challenge for black business owners. It also is one of the key principles of *CITI*works and The 5% Solution Strategy, which emphasize that business owners must remember that when they do 5 percent of their business with other black businesses or black organizations, those businesses and organizations should be *capable* businesses and organizations. *CITI*works and The 5% Solution Strategy contend that if black business owners do business with each other just because they are black they fall into a plantation mentality I call the Post Traumatic Slavery Syndrome.

Introducing community value-add or shared prosperity

Local communities in every city know what is valuable to them and what isn't. Consequently, these local communities may not achieve an outcome determined by groups outside the community because that outcome is not what the community desires or what the community believes is a shared prosperity. In cases such as this, the proposed outcome has no value to the community.

*CITI*works and The 5% Solution Strategy enable local leaders to achieve successful specific market opportunities for their unique communities through a concept called Community Economic Value Add (CEVA). CEVA gives communities the ability to determine their own goals to achieve a specific measurable outcome. Under the CEVA model, even the measurements are self determined. The secret to the success of CEVA is that it changes the language. Instead of being written in a social context, it is written in economic terminology of jobs produced, taxes paid, and benefits derived. This type of language is actually easy for everyone to understand because it hits so close to home. Even people in the barbershop or beauty parlor can recognize how a new contract with the black firm down the street will produce ripples downstream that probably will benefit them through job creation, increased spending by the owners and new employees or in other ways.

I call this change in language "CEO speak." Every corporate CEO understands common business terminologies they use to describe and foretell their concerns. For example, when a new plant moves to your state, the newspaper headline reads "XXXX corporation to create 100 new jobs." Notice that there is no personal identification! However, when black businesses do something similarly significant, headlines in black newspapers will read "Joe Hudson wins contract." CEO language would say the Hudson Group is bringing or retaining 50 jobs to the community. The point of *CITI*works and The 5% Solution Strategy is that the focus must be on the outcome of the transaction, not on the transaction. In this case, the news is that the contract will cause jobs to be created, not that the contract was awarded.

CEVA is a set of outcome measures that are self determined and are a result of a self-designed plan. Because The 5% Solution Strategy is self designed and is built upon black business self reliance, it becomes a self-determining economic opportunity and provides the foundation for community development.

1. The action of creating inner-city growth and development is a deliberate investment through spending and other means in black and other inner-city businesses to produce an inexhaustible economic engine for stabilization and growth.
2. The idea is that value (real or perceived) is created when the return on the entire community opportunity for stabilization and growth is greater, through an active recognized strategic approach, than the negative impact of allowing inner-city communities to lie fallow waiting for the government to step in and solve their problems.
3. The objective is job creation and the stimulation of revolving economic activities caused by black businesses.
4. Efforts undertaken through *CITI*works and The 5% Solution Strategy can be combined with other economic initiatives.

What matters are results

Let's use this metric — Community Economic Value Add/Return on Investment (CEVA/ROI) for measuring minority business contracting success. Why? It's not the contract that matters. It's the *result* of the contract that is important.

This metric is different from the historical standard, which has traditionally relied on a description of social value as a result of affirmative action to demonstrate that minorities were involved in the contracting process. It is the same principle behind describing the contract won by a black or minority firm, which is to specifically mention the owner by name so there is no misunderstanding about the identity or ethnicity of the winner. This form of standard language also served as the backbone for set-aside programs and other entitlement programs.

Today, we see this played out daily in the new healthcare law that requires all Americans to have health insurance. Disclaimers, detractors, and others who do not like the law or the president derisively call the law, officially known as the Patient Protective and Affordable Care Act, "Obamacare." They are using personal identification with President Obama to reframe the name of the bill to distance themselves from it and to point out that he is "not one of them."

Social Value is exhibited by stating the dollar value of a contract and who won the contract. On-the-other-hand, Economic Value portrays the ROI of a contract and how the results from it are measured in jobs created and/or sustained and payroll, income, and other taxes paid. Further, the contract had no relationship with the community nor was input into the process received from the community. The CEVA/ROI response articulates why the programs are necessary and how they lift up those segments of the community where the contractors' business and the employees are located, even if those are in different places.

Why are black businesses valuable?

Because of the affinity of blacks for the black community no matter where the black business happens to be, when black people buy from other black people they address the needs of the black community. Black businesses, which make up a fairly large percentage of the businesses located in an inner-city community, have the ability, skill, and talent plus the respect of the community to take full advantage of the community's assets. This does not mean, however, that black businesses take from the community rather than give back to it. Quite the contrary. Black businesses give back to the community by paying a type of "rent" that supports the community in numerous ways.

Black businesses pay rent by:
a) Creating jobs and hiring local people.
b) Collecting and paying taxes (payroll, sales, unemployment, and similar taxes).
c) Serving as sales/collections agents for lotteries and other statewide initiatives.
d) Supporting other black businesses by doing business with them.
e) Making philanthropic gifts and donating to black-owned and community institutions.

Rent creates a variety of economic benefits for inner-city community, such as:
1. Wages and benefits, including retirement plans for owners and employees.
2. Dividends for the community, such as stability and opportunity for growth.
3. Property value enhancement.
4. Support for bankers and other lenders through the repayments of obligations.
5. Taxes, through payments to governments.
6. Community investments and donations through support for local infrastructure, health, education, and social organizations.
7. Job creation through the hiring of local employees and providing contracts for goods and services to local and regional businesses.
8. Direct and indirect economic value by engaging in activities that help other economic sectors grow, particularly those in inner-city communities.

The offer of a competitive advantage

Black businesses want to be in or near the inner city because this location puts them closest to the densest concentration of their customers and gives them a geographic competitive advantage. Neither the black business community nor cities as a whole have fully exploited this concept as a business strategy. Atlanta is a case in point. The capital city of Georgia and the de facto capital city of the South is regarded as the No. 1 city in America for black business. Neither the business nor the political leaders in Atlanta, however, have pursued the competitive advantage available to them.

This is somewhat surprising. Without a great deal of effort, they could parlay this opportunity into an economic development campaign that would benefit the entire community. Specifically, black business organizations could step up and represent black businesses on the larger playing field of citywide as well as regional economic development. As such, they could partner with local and regional political powers and prominent national black business owners to lead recruiting trips to attract black businesses to Atlanta.

This is where *CITI*works and The 5% Solution Strategy come into play. With statistics showing that two-thirds of employees tend to reflect the ownership, who will gain the majority of these jobs? Blacks, of course. The problem is that neither the city business leaders who recruited Nabisco, UPS and other corporations to Atlanta nor black business organizations nor black elected officials have made similar offers to large black businesses to entice them to relocate to Atlanta. Thus, black businesses are forfeiting their competitive advantage by not relocating to Atlanta, and the city as a whole is losing the economic benefits these businesses would bring.

Even with acknowledged opportunities such as business relocations, Darren Perkins, a business veteran who has spent his career studying, mastering, and implementing business management strategies, writes in his book, "*Business is War the Unfinished Business of Black America*," that the black community has two distinct values that give it a competitive advantage: Black culture and black purchasing power.

Black culture

Blacks have not fully realized there is another aspect to their competitive advantage. They have something that everyone else wants: A distinct style of music and entertainment. These are cultural advantages.

Blacks have a way of initiating cultural change long before their creations and ideas became famous in the non-black market place. For example, all of my friends used to put hot sauce or vinegar on chips and potato skins or mix various flavors of Kool-Aid to get a mixed-fruit taste. Have you looked at store shelves lately? We also made skate boards and scooters before they were mass manufactured. We even died or colored our shoes different colors before Nike was a brand. We used stockings and doo-rags long before these became an accepted part of sports clothing. My uncle drank gin and orange juice years before Seagram's started bottling and selling it and aiming sales pitches at women and light drinkers. These things are a part of the black experience, and they contribute to the black culture. Did you know that "rap" has become bigger in the white market than in the black? Black culture has been adopted for ages in mainstream America, and I imagine it will continue to do so. Black culture can lead to tourism opportunities for the inner-city community and black businesses. That's important because tourism creates as many as 1 in 10 jobs. Also, people of all ages can participate in tourist activities.

Black entrepreneurs and business owners should view the black market and African-American culture as a brand with enormous economic potential. Blacks would be missing a great opportunity if they did not fill this vacuum with distinctive black products and services. They need to create businesses that fill the world's hunger for creative and intellectual properties. If they fail to do this, they can rest assured that a copycat non-black enterprise surely will.

Blacks could create black tourism markets using their culture as a drawing card. These markets could become destinations for tourists and locals that would produce jobs and revenue that would become drivers for the local economy. Existing businesses would grow and expand and new businesses that would be compatible with the new attraction would be created. For example, the re-creation of a former black landmark could be almost as simple as a business stand complete with visual markers. The selling point would be the history/story of what happened there, even though the original landmark is long gone. It is worth noting that international visitors are anxious to hear about the black experience in America.

Black purchasing power

Blacks spend most of their money on:
- Phone services
- Utilities
- Apparel
- Footwear
- Groceries
- Other consumables

Numbers tell the story of black purchasing power.
1. $1 billion annually on boys' clothing, 75 percent more than whites spend on boys' clothing.
2. $500 million per year at McDonald's.
3. 32 percent of all malt liquor products are bought by blacks, who account for 20 percent of purchases in the scotch whiskey market.
4. 10 percent of the $12 billion athletic shoe market is attributed to spending by black males between the ages of 13 and 24, even though they make up less than 3 percent of the U.S. population.
5. 20 percent of Nike shoes are purchased by blacks.
6. $600 million of the $4 billion cosmetics industry is the result of spending by black women, who account for approximately 6 percent of the U.S population. Black women also spend 26 percent more on perfume than any other group of women.
7. $400 million in toothpaste purchases are made by blacks.

Industries in which blacks dominate spending, such as health and beauty aids and alcoholic beverages, suggest areas in which there are business opportunities that entrepreneurs can exploit. What if blacks started to develop businesses not as a mom and pop enterprise but as businesses built to scale using black investment dollars or angel investors? This would require a different type of business plan, but it could be done.

What type of business plan would be needed? It would have to be one that:
1. Understands that blacks need to marshal some of their purchasing power and start producing some of the things they are already buying.
2. Clearly points out where the market is.

3. Shows how to gain market share or dominate it.
4. Shows how to have minimize risk and how to increase ROI.

The economic return to the community is obvious. Whereas these businesses hire both black and white employees, they will employ more blacks than non-blacks. Black hiring, of course, supports inner-city economic development. Salaries from these jobs increase the tax bases of cities and lead to a turnover of the black dollar within the black community.

*CITI*works and The 5% Solution Strategy *won't* work because America has an African-American president. *CITI*works and The 5% Solution Strategy *will work* because they are a strategy that says blacks are no longer a pawn in someone else's game. Economics is an essential part of the foundation of any culture or nation. Powerful economics means powerful political systems.

This concept may sound like hoak'em to some, but it is an idea that has been tried successfully before, albeit in different ways, and it can be done successfully again. When African-Americans put their minds and energy toward a common goal, they can achieve great things. Even though white America has seen it wiser to allow black participation in their system of dominance, it is none-the-less their system and is designed for their advantage. Until they begin to recognize the economics of the black business community, they will continue to ignore black businesses.

Politics aside, the black community is a market and should be treated as such. That's its real value. It also happens to contain many resources important to tapping marketplace success.

Measurements in Economic Impacts

Economic impact studies must be conducted periodically to determine the impact of The 5% Solution Strategy on community social and economic well-being and to determine whether and where mid-course corrections might be needed. The 5% Solution Strategy allows for an analysis that measures both quantitative and qualitative impacts. Quantitative impacts can be evaluated in terms of changes in community demographics, housing, employment and income, market effects, public services, and aesthetic qualities of the community. Qualitative assessments will help identify potential business equity issues, evaluate the adequacy of business services and determine whether the project may adversely affect overall community well-being.

We can't begin to measure success, though, until we get past the race of the business owner. A perception in the black business community is that governments, businesses, and other entities see themselves as taking an undo risk when engaging with black businesses because they consider black business to be marginal businesses. Apparently, black businesses make this assumption because black businesses may initially have less capital than non-black businesses or the business owner may be an entrepreneur with limited experience. While the start-up consideration may have some validity, the experience of the entrepreneur is often vastly underestimated. A study I conducted revealed, for example, that the median work experience of the black entrepreneur is more than eight years, a majority of black entrepreneurs have a college degree and a growing number of them have earned a masters degree. However, the achievements and experiences of black business owners are rarely mentioned. Consequently, misperceptions that blacks are high-risk entrepreneurs continue to fester despite the changing landscape of black entrepreneurship.

Another factor that often is not considered is that The 5% Solution Strategy is an Investment Strategy based on consumer spending. Therefore, the strategy is very risk averse. The overall measure of success is built upon outcomes that occur when the business grows through increased sales. This, of course, is no different than how any business growth pattern would be measured. The only difference is emphasis! It is an investment in which the ROI is defined in a way that all of the stakeholders, including the community, can understand.

Getting these issues on the table and dealing with them is important. This process enables us to establish goals that we can use as a benchmark to measure whether our effort is producing the jobs and other benefits we are striving for. Once the goals are set, we can conduct periodic economic impact studies that will allow us to track different types of critical economic data such as jobs created, where the jobs are located, taxes of all types paid and contributions to local organizations. The numbers will tell us whether we are on the right track or whether we need to make course corrections.

The important thing to remember from the impact studies is that the purpose of the numbers is not for scorekeeping. This is not a game! The purpose of the data is to measure performance. The data reflects the ability of black businesses to provide economic benefits and leadership within the black community for the mutual benefit of the community.

As the late Congressman Adam Clayton Powell said in *"My Black Position Paper,"* "Black masses must produce and contribute to the economy of this country in the proportionate strength of their population." He also said, "Black people must discover a new and creative involvement with ourselves."

Most of the current methods of solving problems in the inner city focus on making changes in the human condition. That is the ultimate goal of *CITI*works and The 5% Solution Strategy as well. But, the way *CITI*works and The 5% Solution Strategy achieve that goal is by changing the economic condition of inner-city residents. For example, *CITI*works and The 5% Solution Strategy offer job training as the primary path to overcoming individual deficiencies.

*CITI*works and The 5% Solution Strategy emphasize job training because income from even low-level jobs offers a better possibility for a "living wage" than do unemployment or other handouts from the government. *CITI*works and The 5% Solution Strategy recognize that job training is a continuing need in the modern workforce. As technology continues to change, more training will inevitably be needed so that workers can maintain the skills needed to stay employed. While job training per se will not create a path to entrepreneurship and economic self sufficiency, the business environment *CITI*works and The 5% Solution Strategy will create will lead to obtaining the skills and, possibly, management development activities that will offer tracks to business ownership.

Black business ownership, however, does offer the opportunity to create wealth for those who are willing to take the risk. Wealth creation can lead to inter-generational wealth and provide the ultimate long-range answer to community development. Why not take advantage of the entrepreneurial opportunities that *CITI*works and The 5%Solution Strategy offer? Others have done so quite successfully. Research shows that black businesses are growing at a rate three times that of other ethnic groups. Perhaps one reason more blacks don't become entrepreneurs is because of what they see as a lack of choice. When no one else will hire you and you have to eat, entrepreneurship might seem like some type of a "hustle" and crime, sadly, becomes the easier, though wrong and more difficult, road.

9 reasons why *CITI*works and The 5% Solution Strategy will work in your city or town

No matter whether you live in a large city or a small town, *CITI*works and The 5% Solution Strategy will:

1. Demonstrate the built-in responsibility that black business have to improve conditions in their communities (which is the same responsibility that other businesses have to the community!) and the economic power of black businesses to live up to that responsibility.

2. Eliminate the notion that black businesses provide no "real value" but have become "wards of the state' that need to be propped up by monetary support from state and federal governments. At the same time it will provide a reason to support black businesses as a viable economic instrument.

3. Move the conversation from one that is centered around social issues with implications of "social engineering" to one about how to use black businesses as a hub to create economic development that will lead to long-term success for the black community.

4. Provide guidelines to show that this approach is a plausible way to use black businesses as an economic tool and a resource for community leadership that will work in any community.

5. Show at its heart how this method is a self-development tool that can be used by both businesses and organizations and once in place will establish a track record of success that will inspire future generations to embrace its methodology.

6. Create incentives for a Return on Investment that will improve life in the black community.

7. Offer black businesses the geographical advantage of "clustering" in a single inner-city location.

8. Give communities and their citizens an "as is" opportunity to begin working to improve versus the alternative of waiting-for-a-better day approach.

9. Demonstrate how the inner city can be a contributor to the economic development of the entire city that will create a sustainable competitive advantage when comparing cities to each other.

Chapter 5

Call to Action! Implementing *CITI*works and The 5% Solution Strategy

"In any moment of decision, the best thing you can do is the right thing, the next best thing is the wrong thing, and the worst thing you can do is nothing."
                                                                Anonymous

The objective of the *CITI*works implementation strategy is to establish value for stakeholders. The 5% Solution Strategy provides a transparent methodology to see and measure that value. It also addresses three easily understood spending and ROI opportunities. They are:

- The ability of black people and black entities to direct spending toward black businesses.
- The ability of black culture and spending to impact black markets.
- The ability of corporate and government supply chains to improve life in the black community.

A seven-step implementation plan

Couple these opportunities with the potential of black people, black organizations and government to direct spending toward black businesses through the principles of *CITI*works and The 5% Solution Strategy, and one will recognize how the Black Dollar can drive community change and revitalization. To achieve the goals of a *CITI*works plan and 5% Solution Strategy for your community, I suggest a seven-step implementation plan based on the points below:

1. Create a *CITI*works Strategy with a new offer to the community.
2. Create a campaign to implement and promote The 5% Solution Strategy.
3. Host at least one public meeting a year to report on the results of the plan and to seek input from the community.
4. Collect and report data on websites or in other forums available to the public.
5. Continually widen ecosystem participation.
6. Ensure black business involvement at ALL levels.
7. Establish a management organization the community will embrace as a "Trusted Agent."

Let's look at how to develop and implement each of these seven steps.

Step One: Create a *CITI*works plan that articulates a "new offer"

This is probably the most important and difficult step because it requires not only that *CITI*works proponents create an action plan, but that they build the plan around new concepts to solving old problems. The plan must contain at least four parts:

1. Goals and objectives: What do you want to achieve? The outcome should be defined in measurable numbers (i.e. 500 jobs from local business during the next 3 years).
2. Value proposition: This expresses what is important to your community (i.e. their values). This is critical because it is what will keep community members involved over time.
3. Resources: What are the important tools, resources, and actions that will be required to reach the plan's goals? These critical elements of the plan must be in constant use and work well all of the time for the plan to succeed. This is where The 5% Solution

Strategy comes into play, along with new and different uses of traditional tools. This portion of the plan offers plan administrators an opportunity to think outside the box by asking themselves: Are there new ways to use the community infrastructure to drive different outcomes than have been achieved in the past using old and out-dated models?
4. Community adjustments: This is where funding may be required as the cost for some adjustments may not have been included in community budgets. Plan administrators should consider the possibility of obtaining funding from non-traditional sources. (i.e. a small business incubator that may want to assist in business development).

The plan MUST be developed using ALL available community resources (more on that later). Collaboratively developed plans are commonly known as a Community Benefits Plan/Agreement. When creating the plan, the focus should be on clarity, inclusiveness, enforceability, and accountability. Be patient! Creating such a plan may take months.

Successful plans, and this is paramount, must give specifics, not generalities. As such, consider following these guidelines when writing the plan:

- Who will drive plan completion? Qualities to look for in a leader include:
    - Personal leadership abilities.
    - Organizational skills.
- How to update and maintain the plan.
- How to implement the plan.
- Public distribution.
- Participant roles and expectations.

These guidelines require the business community to create an organizational structure and name a leadership team that will commit to staying on point as they develop and implement the plan. The structure should focus on the community, its current situation, its aspirations, and the changes businesses and the community must be willing to make to achieve their goals.

Step Two: Create a 5% Solution Strategy promotion and implementation campaign

The campaign should constantly educate the black as well as the entire community about the efforts to produce a new outcome with a new instrument through these operational values:

- Use as wide a model of inclusion as possible.
- Understand your market so you can understand your opportunities that may be unique to your situation.
- Develop a local strategy so you can respond to opportunities.
- Utilize the highest quality services and products at all times.
- Support, sustain and grow the economic value of African-American businesses to the community.
- Support ways of creating intergenerational wealth through business ownership.
- Support contributions to the general health and welfare of the local community, such as

employment of community residents.
- Support the education of African-American consumers, business owners and organizations.
- Support community resources and organizations as partners in the process

Remember, this is a totally different approach to community development. It will take time for everyone has to become accustomed to it and to begin to recognize its outcomes.

Step Three: Host at least one public meeting a year

The meetings should provide a forum to (1) discuss issues that have surfaced since the last meeting and (2) new initiatives to sustain the same level of benefits or to provide improved benefits. The best benefits are usually those that the community can recognize. This forum also lends itself to discussing new initiatives.

It is very important to involve members of your ecosystem, such as leaders in the city as well as the broader community, who initially might not see themselves as important to your plan. Reaching out to include these people will give plan administrators an opportunity to demonstrate that the effort to support black businesses will benefit the entire community and is in no way some under-handed and secretive segregationist ploy.

Perhaps the most important message you can send in planning and hosting regular public meetings is to structure them so that they involve all elements of the community and so they permit everyone to be seen as being on the same level. By doing this you will show that everyone in the community, including small business owners, are seen as full community participants and that everyone, regardless of personal wealth or the size and revenues of their business, is equally important. Panelists and speakers who want to use the meeting to demonstrate their superiority should be avoided. The meetings must be a level playing field!

Step Four: Collect and report data

You must develop and report economic data to document your success and demonstrate the progress that is being made. The data will shorten the negative discourse that is sure to emerge as you work through this project.

Consider beginning your project with an economic impact study. Such a study will provide a base line for your project. Future impact studies can then use this "floor" as a starting point to measure the success of your plan.

Data gathering should involve economic leadership either through local universities or by hiring of an economist. In addition to economic impact studies, information from wage and hourly studies are among the types of data that can be collected.

Step Five: Keep widening ecosystem participation

At the beginning, this project almost by necessity will require that the steering committee be limited to a small group of people. The reason the initial leadership should be limited in numbers is because no one has done this type of continuing education program before and, therefore, only a small group of people will be accustomed to the language you are using and the outcomes you are framing.

However, as the project moves forward, it is important to continually add others from the broader community to the steering committee. As you add people from the larger community, it is imperative for them to understand the overall community benefit of the project and how this effort will create a competitive advantage over other cities in such areas as recruiting business to relocate to your city.

Step six: Ensure black business involvement at all levels

This is where being mindful of the community environment presents new opportunities. We still haven't reached a point in America where black business owners are automatically included in planning for local community development. *CITI*works and The 5% Solution Strategy contend that the local black business community and their allies must be vigilant in involving black business owners in community development planning not for the traditional reasons of creating wealth opportunities but because they are an important instrument of the community.

Black business owners must be included in the planning process of major economic events, as well as actively involved in community projects. This is especially important with civic projects, where the intended outcome and promise is local jobs and other economic benefits. We can't lose sight of the historical reality that under previous civic improvement models the result has been to take the outcome of transactions out of the local community.

Step seven: An organization as a "Trusted Agent"

This may be the most important part of the *CITI*works and The 5% Solution Strategy. It may also be the most difficult to "get right." Establishing a management organization with members that people in the community know and trust to keep the plan alive and to update it as needed is critical to achieving objectives. This organization will require funding to have a staff, but the funding should not come from the government. Ideally, funding should come from the black community, including black foundations and other organizations involved with philanthropy. Its members must be experienced business people or have long ties to the community rather than being well-intentioned folks who lack business, political or social ties. Otherwise, it will take too long for them to "get their legs" before they can perform adequately. They must also be seen as trustworthy and not out for themselves, understand the community, and capable of developing the holistic concept of community. Finally, the organization must perform two other critical acts: (1) It must report regularly to the various stakeholders and the community about data it collects as well as other critical matters and (2) it must conduct audits that will validate planned outcomes.

A new day and a new offer

*CITI*works and The 5% Solution Strategy represent a new offer to American cities and black communities based not just on history but also on economic factors and reality. Simply stated, here's how a community can invest in itself by launching The 5% Solution Strategy through spending choices that will turn over the Black Dollar again and again.

- Each year, every person, organization and business must commit to increase annual spending with black businesses by 5 percent over the previous year.
- Then each black business must increase its spending with other black businesses as well as its community support by 5 percent year over year.
- Each black civic/social/philanthropic organization must also increase its spending and contributions with the black community by 5 percent on an annual basis.

The broad objective, of course, is to create jobs and wealth in the black community and to support the needs of the community by intentionally turning over the Black Dollar as many times as possible within the black community before that dollar exits the community.

Obtaining desired outcomes will require that administrators of the *CITI*works and 5% Solution Strategy create a new set of local rules to implement their plan. These new rules must not only be different from the rules of previous civic improvement models, they must educate the community about the new model and involve the community in implementing them. Here are three key points to keep in mind when creating the new rules:

- The current rules were designed by the majority community and as such were designed to support the needs of the white community.
- The new rules will be designed by the local community to produce a group economic outcome.
- The new rules must indicate support for the entire community as an employment base but focus on the black community because *a rising tide raises ALL ships.*

Black people can bank the profits of *CITI*works

*CITI*works asks the black community to collectively ask itself three questions:

    A. Why do you pour your money into non-black enterprises that make *no* contribution to the black community?
    B. Why do you let non-blacks sell your black culture back to you?
    C. Why do you let the opponents of black self help and minority business defeat the programs that would allow black people to gain a larger share of the American dream?

By recognizing the power of black culture, the economic wealth that already exists in some segments of the black community and the strength of the Black Dollar, the black community can create and promote black businesses that will keep black and non-black consumers demanding more and more products and services from black businesses. And black business owners and the black people they will employ can bank the profits! If black people will just watch where they spend their dollar and commit to spending 5 percent more with black businesses every year, they can create the jobs and add to the coffers of their governments, thereby improving services provided to them, while realizing a better return on the investment they make in their community than they have ever received in the past.

As we look out for ourselves, remember these four things and let them sustain you:

1. **This is our money and the black community is our market, though not a market that thinks of itself as privileged.**
2. **These are our business, our consumers and our institutions.**
3. *CITI*works **and The 5% Solution Strategy are not a set-aside or a form of affirmative action.**
4. **This is not a social program or an entitlement. It is a business program.**

Therefore black-inner city communities do not need permission to implement *CITI*works and The 5% Solution Strategy. Why? Because black people are using their assets to help black businesses help the black community. We have the cash, talent, tools and now a plan with a process. We just have to set our minds to it! When we do that, we will empower black businesses to lead, implement and become beneficiaries of a system that will enhance the development of black communities and create jobs for black people that will benefit not only the black community but the entire city.

Conclusion

When implementing *CITI*works and The 5% Solution Strategy, communities must decide where the plan will reside and who will manage it. This effort is a long-term strategy that is far from almost any form of instant gratification. Even when some things are immediately available, they must be thought about in terms of how they will benefit this plan years into the future. It is important to also keep in mind that the results may not always be the same ones that were originally intended.

This possible situation points out one of the major problems about community resources, which is that they often are driven by the objective of the person who funds them rather than the goal of the recipient. Implementing the *CITI*works model will redirect many resources from their original intent, which in and of itself will be a major challenge. The goal is for the resources to help produce results that will have meaningful and lasting impact.

The *CITI*works model also offers the opportunity to insert measurements and metrics to help determine whether the plan is on schedule. For example, if the plan calls for (x) number of meetings per month and there are but half that number, the community can readily recognize the plan is behind schedule. This plan demands accountability to and from the community.

Experience has taught me that plans, no matter how well thought out, do not always unfurl systematically as intended. Some things happen easily. Others must be cobbled together. This is why there must be an accountable plan manager who keeps everybody focused and on schedule through regular status reports. Who that person will be is a major decision. It should not, however, be government in any form but an organization led by black businesses. Finally, the group leading the plan must move it from the planning stage to a recognized campaign to make the community aware of it.

It is very important that the majority community understand the *CITI*works effort and not think of leaders of the plan as separatists. They must understand the goal of the plan is to develop and sustain the black community. With black businesses becoming leaders in the development of strategies to support the black community, they are relieving the larger community of the responsibilities for the inner city that they assumed in the past. The entire effort will take years of hard work and dedication. It will be worth it, though. For in the 21st century, white support has withdrawn and is prioritized elsewhere. "The cavalry ain't coming," and we must fend for ourselves.

Section four

What others are saying

"At the end of the day, what is good for black communities, and all communities of color, strengthens the American economy and allows the United States to remain globally competitive."
Daryl Williams – Kauffman Foundation

What others are saying about black businesses

"**The black community is soldering** its way through an economic calamity. More than a quarter of all black Americans are poor, as are more than a third of all black children. Doors of economic opportunity— in the workforce, in access to higher education, and elsewhere — are slamming shut at a breathtaking rate. It is futile to view the desperate struggle of African-American businesses outside the context of two overwhelming imperatives: The obligation of the United States to figure out how to put its population to work in jobs that will support families and sustain a world-class economy; and the parallel obligation, perpetually avoided, to bring black Americans and all of their talent and energy fully into the fold of the wider society"

Bob Herbert

"**Many black communities are suffering** from unemployment, underemployment and many other negative economic indicators that impact the quality of life for individuals living in these communities. Given that recent models of economic transformation do not appear to be yielding the desired results for black communities, maybe it's time to re-evaluate some historical perspectives on how best to bring economic prosperity to black communities.

According to James Clingman Jr. in a 2010 article titled "*Buying Black - the Ebony Experiment*," $850 billion is moving through black consumers' hands each year, with 90 percent of that amount going to businesses owned and controlled by non-black businesses. That is a vast amount of revenue that never makes its way to the African-American community. Could there be a connection between the economic health of a community and the amount of money spent in the businesses within that community by its residents? Examples of successful ethnic enclave models around the country suggest that, at some level, residents within a community do indeed economically enhance that community when there is a significant amount of patronage of local businesses. Given the severe poverty and bleak economic reality found in many black communities, it might make sense to examine the strategies that parallel this concept and helped produce it, according to Juliet E.K. Walker's *"The History of Black Business in America, the Golden age of Black Business From 1900-1930."*

This sounds like the "double duty dollar" concept from the early 1990's! The double-duty dollar concept holds that if black consumers buy goods and services from black-owned businesses, the dollars spent have a doubling effect: the spending power of the dollars being transferred from the black consumer to the lack business owner. This "doubling" effect creates an additional flow of capital within a community that has significant impact on new opportunities, jobs and local businesses. Does this strategy have relevance in the current efforts to revitalize African-American communities throughout the country? If Clingman's math is correct, $765 billion spent by black consumers never touches black businesses or the black community. Perhaps the reduction of the 90 percent "dollar flight" from black communities could be a significant catalyst to improve the quality of life and economies in black communities throughout the United States.

"John and Maggie Anderson examined this question with their "Ebony Experiment," which consisted of a year-long commitment to purchase all of their goods and services from black-owned businesses. Can this double-duty dollar concept be revisited or should it even be considered? There are numerous ethnic enclaves throughout the country that do a high level of business among community members. Many of these communities have healthy local economies and understand the importance of supporting businesses located where they reside. However, for this concept to have any traction in black communities, businesses have to provide quality services and products as well as creatively integrate themselves in the community. Sponsorships, mentoring, leading community improvement projects and philanthropic activities are just a few innovative ways businesses can be a value-add to a community. This is important because communities, consumers and businesses must all get value for their efforts in this concept of reciprocity.

This is not to suggest that blacks only buy from black-owned businesses. Also, it is not realistic for African-Americans to make all their purchases from black-owned businesses. America should be a country where goods and services are consumed from businesses that provide the highest quality and value regardless of ethnic origin. Still, any percentage of the $765 billion spent outside of black communities could make a significant impact on some of the economic issues currently facing many black communities. At the end of the day, what is good for black communities, and all communities of color, strengthens the American economy and allows the United States to remain globally competitive. Therefore, in the spirit of Black History Month, maybe we should take a minute to examine current problems through a historical lens and look at the solutions that have been offered by some of the great minds of the past. Perhaps these voices can inform us of how to best proceed in the times we now face. As Edmund Burke warns us, "Those who don't know history are destined to repeat it."

Daryl Williams – Kauffman Foundation

"**Black communities need to grow**; they must fulfill social, psychological, and commercial needs. A community should adequately provide the means for moving goods, people, and information, and allow for maximum freedom of choice on interaction among residents while providing safety and comfort. We need structures where we can live, work, shop and play that are harmonious and contextual. Black entrepreneurs must begin to build a world they want to live in. We should have places to shop, dine and live within our communities. We should not have to go out into other ethnic communities to do these things."
Darren Perkins – *"Business is War—The Unfinished Business of Black America"*

Section five

Black spending power: statistical data

"You can't lead the Calvary if you think you look funny on a horse"
Anonymous

CITIworks and The 5% Solution Strategy

How black business impacts the economy

Here is a snapshot of the impact of black businesses on the national economy and a look at the impact of black businesses on local and state economies, using Atlanta and Georgia as an example.

The national economy

• During a recent five-year period, black businesses out-grew businesses of all other ethnic groups.
• For every $1 million spent with black businesses, 10 jobs are added to the business; 7 of those go to blacks.
• Every $1 million of Black Business revenue adds $3.1 million in to total US output and 25 jobs to the economy.
• Black businesses operate in neighborhoods that are 44 percent black.
• 35 percent of black businesses are located in high poverty areas.
• Black businesses doubled in number between 1992 and 2002.
• Black businesses are growing at a rate of nearly three times that of all other minority groups.
• Increasing the capacity and competitiveness of black-owned firms is the most important imperative for our community and country.
• Black businesses account for a growing percentage of jobs.
• Black businesses tend to be located in underserved communities.
• The most preferred city in the United States to locate a black business is Atlanta.
• 95 percent of Black Dollars are spent outside the black community
• Every dollar spent creates $2.2 in business activity.

Source: Dr. Thomas Boston, president of EuQuant and professor of economics at Georgia Institute of Technology in Atlanta.

Atlanta, the metro area and Georgia

Atlanta is the No. 1 choice among blacks to open a business in the United States. Black businesses and black spending have a significant impact on the economy of the city, the region and the state.

- There are approximately 115,000 black businesses in metro Atlanta.
- Black businesses have a $24 billion impact on the metro area.
- Black Businesses employed more than 52,000 people and stimulate the employment of an additional 166,000 in 2007.
- Black consumers in metro Atlanta spend in excess of $28B annually.
- Economic Impact on Region: $8 billion
- Overall Impact on Jobs: 26K
- Impact on Jobs: 82K (Jobs Spawned by)
- Impact on Earnings: $2.8 billion
- Estimated Impact 2007
- Economic Impact: $23.5 billion
- Overall impact on jobs: 219,000

- Direct impact on jobs: 52,000
- Impact on earnings: $7 billion
- Direct sales: $10.7 billion
- $37.6 billion in output in buying power estimated 2010
- 1 percent increase in buying power = $376M

Source: Atlanta Business League Economic Impact Study by Dr. Edward Davis, Bead Business School at Atlanta University.

- Black spending statewide was projected to be $54 billion in 2007.
- Georgia is the fourth largest African-American market in the United States.
- Atlanta is third in (2002) in the number of black businesses
- Black buying power in metro Atlanta is projected at] $28 billion for 2007.
- Black population is growing at faster rate than that of whites or ethnic groups in the United States.
- Blacks comprise 22 percent of the buying power in metro Atlanta.
- Georgia is No. 4 in black buying power in the United States/

Source: Selig Center, University of Georgia.

Census report

- Black population of metro Georgia: 2.3 million.
- Georgia has the fifth largest black population in the United States.
- The median income of blacks in Georgia is $31,000.
- Black population of metro Atlanta: 1.2 million

Published by
The Hudson Strategic Group
6856 Tara Oaks Drive
Riverdale, GA 30274
770-994-4466

Information on Mr. Hudson
www.josephrhudson.com
email:jrh@josephrhudson.com
404-281-9545

Mr. Hudson is available for speaking engagements, book signings, panels, workshops, strategic consultations, and community engagement activities

www.ingramcontent.com/pod-product-compliance
Lightning Source LLC
Chambersburg PA
CBHW071747170526
45167CB00003B/974